Undertaken with Love

Under her stage name of Jane Hilary, Jane
Spottiswoode has appeared in many plays and TV
productions including *The Good Life* and *Poldark*.
She played Mrs Darling in *Peter Pan* with Dorothy
Tutin and Eric Porter at the London Coliseum.
   Today Jane Spottiswoode lives near Bala in North
Wales.

Nadine

Thank you so much for your support
during the time we lost John. This
book, in it's own way, also helped
us to cope with his death and
birth as totally natural, beautiful
life events.

I hope you find it as enlightening
and thought provoking as I did.

with much love,

Mary

April 1997

Undertaken with Love

Jane Spottiswoode

ROBERT HALE · LONDON

ISBN 0 7090 4979 X

Robert Hale Limited
Clerkenwell House
Clerkenwell Green
London EC1R 0HT

Photoset in North Wales by
Derek Doyle & Associates, Mold, Clwyd.
Printed in Great Britain by
St Edmundsbury Press, Bury St Edmunds, Suffolk.
Bound by WBC Bookbinders Limited.

Contents

For my fellow 'loving undertakers'
Joy and Alan Byrne

Illustrations

PICTURE CREDITS

Colin Russell: 3. The late Peter Turner: 7. From *Small Beer* by Ludwig Bemelmans (Bodley Head, 1940): 11. David J. Barton: 12.

Acknowledgements

The author wishes to thank the following for permission to reproduce written material:

Faber and Faber for *Rosencrantz and Guildenstern are Dead* by Tom Stoppard.

Grove Press for *Inability to Mourn* by Alexander and Margarette Mitscherlich.

Methuen Childrens Books for *Winnie the Pooh* by A.A. Milne.

Stephen Pile for a quote from an article in *The Sunday Times*.

Anthony Smith for a quote from his BBC Radio 4 series *A Sideways Look*.

The author would also like to thank the following for their help, encouragement and belief in the writing of this book:

David Barton, Richard Buckley, Richard Owen Jones, Anthony Caswell, Deryck Humphrey, the late George Smith, Moira Lovell, Mitzi Roberts, Mary-Anne Borwick, J.G. Haughton and everyone who took the trouble to write to her recounting their experiences and to offer their support.

'No one seemed to appreciate that the "body" they were discussing was actually the person I loved.'

Next-of-kin talking of the attitude of some staff in a Birmingham hospital.

Preface

The following is an account of a life and a death. 'Lifestyle' is a well-used – even a jargon – word today, but 'deathstyle' is not. In which case I have perhaps invented it, but I hope to show in the story which follows how one developed quite naturally out of the other.

The first part concerns an endeavour to achieve that late-twentieth-century dream of self-sufficiency, and the frustrations – far outweighed by the joys – in the undertaking. Many, I know, have adopted this way of life but for few, I suspect, was the entire project dependent upon the creation of power from a natural renewable resource, i.e. water. Of the man who achieved this, Nigel Spottiswoode, whose abhorrence of waste motivated much of his life, a fellow water-power enthusiast said, 'It must have given him enormous satisfaction. He could truly say, "I lift up mine eyes to the hills from whence cometh my strength".'

The second part relates how I funeralized Nigel without employing a funeral director, and the complications, implications and consequences of so doing. I am not keen on the verb 'to funeralize', but like many an Americanism from which we traditionalist British initially recoil, it does, nevertheless, express exactly what I did.

I can't say I buried him, because he was cremated, but if I say I cremated him, it sounds as if I, personally, struck the match – with all the connotations of the Joan

11

of Arc story. So I am settling for 'funeralize', because I know of no other word that combines the two methods of disposal.

Looking back on it now, my feelings still vacillate between almost believing my publicity, i.e. that I am a remarkable and admirable woman ('representing everything that is best about the British!' was one comment – and I must admit it was heady stuff) and thinking, 'What the Dickens is all the fuss about?' My husband was merely taken to the crematorium by his friends, instead of employing a stranger to do it. That was all it amounted to, really, and if more people realized how comparatively easy it can be with a little forethought, they might like to consider it themselves.

It was certainly a lot cheaper and a more personal, relaxed and moving affair than the usual ceremony and – at the risk of seeming to trivialize something that is usually solemn and sorrowful – a lot more fun. This is not to say for a moment that we didn't take it seriously. This we most certainly did. It was simply our own kind of serious and not prescribed by others.

Nigel was a conservationist long before the term became fashionable, not just in life but also in death, as I shall recount.

As for me, my dominant feeling is one of triumph that I was able to carry out his plan and also that no one who wasn't a friend touched him from the time he died until the time he went down the chute.

And *that* meant a lot.

1   The Melin

My story has been called 'extraordinary', 'bizarre' and 'surrealist'. It didn't seem so to me, at least not at the beginning: just another frustrating case of the consumer uncatered-for. However, one did need a well-developed sense of the ridiculous – particularly at such a time: you see, my husband, Nigel, was dying.

This is how it happened. Long before, when he was in perfect health, we had watched a television programme concerned with the high cost of dying and had sent for the accompanying booklet, entitled, appropriately, *It's a R.I.P. Off*. This we read with great interest, but at the time my husband merely made enquiries about leaving his body for medical research and was told there was not a teaching hospital near enough to accept him. Apparently the cost of transport would be out of the question when there was a plentiful supply obtainable locally.

He then enquired – not too seriously, I feel – about the practicality of being put bodily on the compost heap, thereby incurring no cost and contributing, in time, to the fertility of the soil. However, our GP persuaded him that such a course would be against the Public Health Act. So there the subject rested for a while, except that we agreed to purchase coffins at some future date to put by in readiness for the inevitable, but owing to the usual pressures of day-to-day living we never got around to it.

Nevertheless the subject was not forgotten, and we

agreed that the average funeral was a complete waste of money which, instead of mourning the dead, should be spent on celebrating their lives. In other words, a jolly good booze-up.

Also we discovered in conversation that we were not the only people who felt that the usual procedure was a wasteful and gruesome affair.

We were, at that time, living in an old water-mill in North Wales, near the small town of Bala. Bala is a big tourist attraction in the summer season – indeed, almost all the year round, mainly because of its lake, which is the largest stretch of natural water in the principality and ideal for many water sports new and old which become more popular every year.

We were both southerners. Nigel had been born and reared in Bath and I in Bushey, Hertfordshire. The reason for our settling where we did was because Nigel, being an electrical and water engineer, had always believed that by the time he reached retirement the world would be starting to run out of power. He had been in the lighthouse business for most of his life and was chief engineer in a firm which also made other marine signals, such as buoys and tide gauges, many of which were his design.

Nigel and I had been together, as the saying goes, for ten or more years, and as he was approaching sixty – at which age he proposed to retire, we had, for more than a year, spent many weekends searching the British Isles for a dwelling with water-power which, with Nigel's expertise, would supply all our heating and lighting needs and, in Nigel's words, 'free us from the vagaries of Scargill and the Oil Sheiks'.

We had spent much time looking for the right place and seemed to have explored almost every corner of the country, from Devon to Cumberland, and had almost settled on a disused mill at Fisherton-de-la-Mare, near Amesbury. We would have had to rebuild practically from scratch but nevertheless my mind was already way

ahead and planning the furnishing and decorating of the
place. It was, therefore, with a certain displeasure, that I
received, one Friday evening, Nigel's announcement that
he had been sent details of a converted mill in Wales and
we'd better drive up the next morning to take a look at it.
I knew it was no use protesting. Nigel had that far-away
look that the words 'water-mill' always produced.

During the journey north I was, I admit, slightly sulky.
Wales, to date, I knew naught of – apart from a week at
Cardiff in *The Maid of the Mountains*, and one at
Swansea with Agatha Christie's *Murder at the Vicarage*,
both appearances as a young actress many years before.
On the first occasion, I remembered, I had found a highly
personable stray kitten and before the week was up had
delivered it to what promised to be a good new home
adjacent to that jokey castle. On the other, the only
memory was that I had chosen as my lodgings, from the
Equity good-digs book, an establishment under the
auspices of a Madam somebody or other, under the
mistaken impression that she was French and therefore
bound to produce the most delicious *cuisine* for which her
country was rightly famous. Wrong! She was a piano
teacher (most piano teachers give themselves the title
Madam in South Wales), and the food was as tasteless as
any I had encountered. These two incidents hardly added
up to a minimal knowledge of the principality.

So there I sat, my mind still in Fisherton-de-la-Mare,
hurtling north-west up the motorway, feeling most
unco-operative. I had hoped that these weekends of
dashing about Britain with estate agents' details in my
lap were a thing of the past.

And then we saw it. Standing back from the lane and
slightly below it, at the bottom of a weed-covered drive.
In fact, the weeds were the most notable feature at first
glance – more than waist-high in places, and Nigel soon
disappeared among them, heading uphill to check the
height of the fall of water, which I had learnt was
described as 'the head'. Nigel never looked at any
building before examining the head, and I had learnt

never to become too enthused about interiors until this
had been done. So this time I wandered round, taking in
the house from the outside. It was far from the idealized
water-mill beloved by greetings-cards and table-mat
manufacturers. Large and uncompromisingly rectangular, it was built of granite, or what is known as granite in
these parts. Attached to the mill was the mill cottage, an
attractive virginia-creeper-covered three-up and three-
down affair, I discovered, having collected the keys as
instructed from the small stable which adjoined it.

A glance inside showed that someone had taken
trouble, and there was a really friendly feeling about the
place. Downstairs, on one side of the front door was a
large sitting-room and on the other a bathroom which
had certainly started life as the front parlour and had
probably been used only on occasions of wedding parties
and funerals. Through the slate-floored living-room, with
its exposed beams, open grate and massive heart-of-oak
mantelpiece, was the kitchen. I noticed the attractive
terracotta-tiled floor and another open fireplace which at
the time housed the refrigerator.

This description, I realize, is starting to sound like the
eulogistic ravings of a highly imaginative estate agent,
but I can't help it. I was in a state of complete
enchantment.

Above my head was a half gallery which I later
discovered had been traditionally the sleeping-quarters
of the miller's apprentice. At this time it was filled with
the sort of junk that might come in handy one day if one
could remember where one had put it.

The back door of the kitchen led out onto a slate-paved
path at the foot of three steep terraces giving much
lebensraum to many varieties of voracious weeds and
scrubby elder bushes. My mind's eye saw it well tamed
and abloom with all kinds of ground-cover plants.
Heathers? Why not? The soil was suitably acid, I
suspected, judging by the proliferation of rhododendrons
I had seen. Stop it, I thought. Nigel wasn't back yet and I
must curb my wilder fantasies.

Continuing along the slate path with the back of the
mill on my left, it widened under a wooden bridge, with
the terraced land on my right. Nigel explained later that
the bridge was where the water had descended from the
millpond onto the wheel, which sadly was no more. On
the top terrace was a line of cypress leylandii trees, quite
small as yet, eight rhododendron bushes – obviously
fairly recent plantings, and on ground level a grinding
stone four feet across which had been set on a granite
plinth and made into a table with slate seats supported
on bricks at right angles to it. A huge, heavy, panelled
oak door faced it, and peering through the windows I saw
that it led into the mill kitchen. Above was a low-walled
sun terrace.

I continued my way around to the front and hesitated.
There were four steps at each end of a loading-bay which
ran the full length of the house. In the centre was inset
yet another millstone seeded with yellow stone-crop. At
each end of the bay, the steps led to a half-glass panelled
front door. I tried a key in the right-hand one. It turned. I
was inside the mill.

The ground floor was tiled, and two-thirds along the
length of this massive forty- by twenty-foot room was a
magnificent fireplace – the chimney breast built of huge
granite stones with access on either side to what was
obviously the dining-area. On one side of this access the
stones had been continued to form an archway which
immediately suggested the childhood joys of caves and
visits to Father Christmas's grotto in the bigger Oxford
Street department stores.

From the dining-area another archway led into the
kitchen, a long, narrow, galley-type room with two deeply
recessed windows – the sills tiled, under one of which was
a modern stainless-steel sink, I was pleased to note.
Continuing on past the huge oak door I had observed
from the outside was another passage leading to a
cloakroom, as the euphemism goes, otherwise a loo and
wash basin and turning right I was back in the main
area.

Opposite the front door I had come in by was a staircase which I proceeded to climb. At the top I found myself in a wide gallery looking down onto the floor below. Ahead of me was a glass-panelled oak door which led out to the sun terrace.

The terrace, I decided, I would investigate later. I walked along the oak-railed gallery, looking both down and up at the magnificent chimney. Until now my only objection to living in a water-mill had been a conviction that it was bound to be dark, water-mills having a habit of being in valleys, Nigel explained, but it was wonderfully light up there, with two large, deep-set windows. Goodness, the walls were thick – nearly three feet deep, I guessed. I was again walking along the length of the building and through another archway into an area with yet two more large windows and another fireplace built into the opposite side of the chimney from the one below, with a raised slate hearth. I had now turned right across the width of the mill where another staircase led up to the top floor. Past it and through yet another archway was a small vestibule, off which was a perfectly adequate bathroom, and another door to the sun terrace. I was pleased to see that the bathroom was fitted with a perfectly conventional door and even a bolt!

I retraced my steps and climbed the second flight of stairs. They rose steeply and led to a fair-sized landing with a bedroom at each end, with a wash basin in each – bliss! The landing itself was fitted with two large, double-glazed skylights in the sloping ceiling, which I now realized were responsible for the light and feeling of airiness throughout the upper floors.

Looking over the oak rails, I could see the gallery floor and, further below, the ground-floor area, the spectacular chimney continuing upward and out of sight above the sloping-beamed ceiling. The walls not of stone had been plastered and whitewashed, with here and there a grey stone protruding where it had been too large or awkward to remove and cover. And that was it – only two bedrooms in all that space.

But then my eye caught a pair of heavy wool embroidered curtains drawn across an angled alcove. Very curious. Further investigation revealed a small space which would nevertheless accommodate a pair of bunk beds, a chest of drawers and a rail for clothes. It also incorporated a tiny iron-framed window with thick bubble-glass panes which opened and closed on nothing in particular. How children would love it – well, this one did anyway. They would probably play that disgusting game of spitting on people from a great height. Such jolly fun at a certain age.

I set off to look for Nigel – quite a long way down, as the staircases didn't connect and one had to walk the complete length of the first-floor gallery before descending the second. This, I must admit, became a bore in time but now nothing could spoil my enchantment. I felt like Dorothy in *The Wizard of Oz* on first seeing Munchkinland – the scene when the screen changed from sepia to glorious Technicolor and Judy Garland spoke that immortal line, 'You know, Toto, I don't believe we're in Kansas any more.'

Crossing again to the fireplace, I gazed at it with awe, and had I been of a religious bent I would have fallen on my knees and prayed that the water would meet Nigel's requirements so that on winter evenings, when we were doing our Darby and Joan bit, we could sit and worship the spirit of the fire, the hearth, the very essence of our home. In most city homes the television is now the focal point of the room, many dwellings being built without a grate at all. How sorry I felt for them as I stood with my images of a future of crackling kindling and bringing the pine logs hither and other rustic carry-ons. The back-to-nature cult had really got me – but with heat and light and hot baths at the turn of a switch. Would we be merely playing at being bucolics, I wondered. No, not really, not if we were creating our own heat and light from natural renewable sources. And I was determined to grow our fruit and vegetables. I was already vegetarian, and Nigel just liked food. That it should be fresh and well cooked was all he asked.

I started dreaming again until I heard footsteps outside. A big grin appeared at the door, followed by the rest of Nigel, his trousers sodden to the waistband. In spite of his expression, my mouth was dry.

'Well?' I said.

'Possibilities,' was the reply. 'Distinct possibilities. How about the house?'

'Come and see for yourself,' I said.

I completed another tour of the mill and cottage, this time with Nigel in tow, trying to sound as objective as I could, as if I, too, saw mere possibilities, but as our tour progressed I could see that Nigel had warmed to it almost as much as I. He pointed out some 'interesting features' that I had missed, such as some of the wooden working parts of the mill machinery set high in the plastered walls, and told me what they had originally been used for. I was disappointed that the water-wheel had gone – the kitchen had been built over the pit which had housed it. It would have been nice to have it, even if not actually turning. I knew Nigel had other plans. Some years before, when he was hunting for a mill in the West Country, and I was on tour with some show or other, he wrote me:

The only wheel I found on this trip is still very much in business, grinding corn on two pairs of stones. With true Devon courtesy the miller abandoned his accounts and we spent the afternoon discussing the relative merits of apple and yew for pit wheel teeth. He conceded that apple was a useful wood, provided the tree had grown cooking apples – the sweeter the apple the softer the wood he said. Earlier in my visit I had spotted some castings on his scrap heap which I was fairly sure belonged to a turbine. Knowing a bit about Devonians I expressed no particular interest but commented on their rustiness and on the difficulty of getting spares for such old equipment. By the time I left, I'd beaten him down to about twice the price he probably had in mind.

He had added that his new possession would need 'a bit of doing up', but other engineers working at Nigel's firm seemed almost as fascinated as he himself, and once it arrived on the premises Nigel remarked jokingly, 'Not too many lighthouses were made for a couple of years.'

So we were really looking for a home for the turbine (which needed a thirty-foot head of water), as well as for ourselves. Nigel assured me that it would be more efficient than the wheel and produce considerably more electricity, and I had to be content with that.

He had once said that he didn't know whether his passion for water-power was a result of meanness or had some deeper Freudian significance. I think I can tell you. It certainly wasn't meanness – he was the most generous of men with his money, his time and his affections. It was abhorrence of waste of any kind of resource that motivated him. He hated to see a dripping tap, and nothing made him angrier than Blackpool Tower blazing with, what to him was, utterly squandered energy.

Back to the moment. Nigel was almost as impressed with the fireplace as I had been, and really it inspired a feeling that was almost reverent. He was particularly delighted by the hearth – a seven-foot-by-three slate slab – probably a gravestone, he thought. It was magnificent and would come up a treat with a rubbing of linseed oil.

We had arranged with the agents that if we were interested we would stay the night in a local hotel and the next day meet the builder who had done much of the reconstruction of the place. He would be there the next morning if summoned, and Nigel could have a general discussion with him and leave him some sums to do regarding the all-decisive head.

The first thing though was to get Nigel into some clean, dry clothes. The White Lion in Bala agreed to accommodate us, and over dinner I was glad to realize that Nigel's fantasies were equalling mine, though of a different nature.

It had always been one of his Walter Mittyisms to run a restaurant, and this we discussed with extreme

earnestness. We would be open in the summer only and
serve the many holiday-makers who swelled the local
population from June until the end of September. There
was a large, two-storey garage that when adapted would
house a couple of students who would wait at table, and
Nigel and I would cook. I would also grow all our own
organic vegetables for the table. We completely ignored
several facts. First, that Nigel would refuse entry to
anyone to whom he took a dislike, and the ones he did
like he wouldn't want to charge, a distinct disadvantage
from a business point of view. Second, that having
worked hard in the acting profession all my life, the last
thing I would enjoy was working the clock round every
summer when I could be sunbathing and swimming in
Bala Lake. Also, it later transpired, the scheme would
have been doomed to disappointment, because we
wouldn't have been granted the necessary planning
permission for change of use. Nevertheless, it was a
sublimely happy evening, although, as we kept reminding each other, 'nothing was settled yet'.

After breakfast we drove back to Melin Meloch, as it
was called. '*Melin*' is Welsh for 'mill', and the Meloch was
the river which ran through the property, from which the
diversion from the weir through the millpond, under the
road and out into the famous River Dee would supply our
needs. 'The weir will last a lifetime,' Nigel said, 'and the
millpond only needs a bit of clearing out.' This proved an
understatement but in essence was true.

The builder, a cheerful Welshman who was justly
proud of his work, met us. We discovered that he,
single-handed, had built that chimney without the use of
mechanical lifting-gear. Our respect knew no bounds. He
described the heap of rubble from which it and the rest of
the building had risen and how he and the owner, who
came up for weekends, had taken eight years to finish it
and turn it into the Mirimar which we now perceived it to
be. Nevertheless, we, probably unsuccessfully, tried to
hide our enthusiasm, in the manner of those who have
several properties to view of which this was only one in

which we felt a mild interest. After all, the genial builder
was still the vendor's representative.

The only problem was that we had envisaged a tumble-
down affair that we would rebuild over the period of time
while we were still living and working in London. But this
place was practically ready to move into, 'Just a few
finishing-off jobs,' Nigel said optimistically. On the other
hand we had watched the dismal faces of friends who were
resuscitating old cottages and who spent their weekends
streaking down to the country to see how the builders
were getting on – and they weren't. But obviously a place
not already converted would cost less initially, and the
price of rebuilding would be spread over a longer period.
We readily agreed that the conversion had been carried
out with more imagination than we would have been able
to bring to it, but could we afford it?

Nigel's comment after first viewing the interior was,
'Well, it's a trifle Hollywood baronial but I like it.'

It was after one o'clock when Nigel finally returned his
notebook to his pocket and we were on our way back to The
Smoke. We'd decided to have a ploughman's lunch or some
such at a likely-looking pub we'd seen in the next village.
Herewith came our first culture shock. It was closed. We
tried the next couple of villages also before the truth
dawned. This area was in one of the five Welsh 'never-on-
Sunday' counties. Back in the car, map out. What and how
far was the next county, and could we make it to the border
before closing-time? The next county was Denbigh, in
those days before the 'bigger-is-better' shuffle took place,
and we arrived there just in time to have the door of the
first pub shut in our faces with the sort of clank against
which pleas and arguments would be obviously unre-
warding. Two hours later and ravenous, we settled for egg
and chips at a motorway service station.

Later that week, back home, the figures regarding the
water, its fall and the general layout of the land arrived,
and Nigel, like God in the creation, saw them and saw that
they were good.

Then began lengthy discussions on ways and means.
We owned no property, as we lived in a rented flat and in
any case needed a home in London for at least two more
years. We were determined not to start off with a
mortgage round our necks if we could possibly avoid it.
We did, however, both have a certain number of
securities, and a good few hours were spent deciding
which to sell. It seemed that we could just about raise the
amount of the offer we had decided upon and still avoid
bankruptcy. We offered.

If ever I was asked what Nigel 'did', I would reply that
he was a designer, or sometimes I'd say an inventor, but
he always spoke of himself as an engineer. This was in no
way false modesty – he considered engineering one of the
highest possible callings. After he died a colleague wrote,

> In the lighthouse field I am sure he will be remembered as
> having made one of the important inventions. He knew,
> as we all did, that power on lighthouses is very expensive
> due to inaccessibility. He realised that the power required
> to rotate an optic, even the large ones, was less than
> anyone had assumed. The significance of his gearless
> pedestal has not yet been fully realised but it so
> influenced engineer's thinking that solar powered lights
> are feasible even in the higher ranges. There is no doubt
> that the significance of his invention will be recognised
> more clearly in due course. These people are rarely
> honoured in their lifetime.

I must say that all this was news to me, but then Nigel
never voluntarily discussed his work at home. When I
have, on occasion, remarked upon this to other company
wives, their reaction has been one of near disbelief,
followed by looks of passionate envy. (Once a 14-year-old
son of a friend asked him if he didn't ever get nervous
building lighthouses with the sea pounding ferociously
on the rocks below him. Nigel explained that he merely
designed the lights, which were installed later. 'Oh, I
see,' said the young man. 'You just put the bulbs in.' Nigel

was delighted. 'Yes, yes,' he said, 'that's exactly what I do. I've never heard it described better!')

In our flat the telephone rang. For the past week I had been learning lines in preparation for an appearance in a new play due to start rehearsing later that month, and I loathed interruptions.

'Is that Mrs Miller?' enquired a male voice.

'No,' I said shortly, 'there's no one of that name here.'

'Hang on a minute, stoopid,' said Nigel in his normal tone. 'We've got it!'

Our offer had been accepted. We were the millers of Melin Meloch. There had never been a moment like it.

So that was how it all began – the life, or rather the new life, or better still the Good Life. (I had a part in that – *The Good Life* TV series, I mean, and proud I was to play it. It must have been almost everybody's favourite comedy series of the time – possibly of all time.)

For the next 2½ years we spent as much time as we could at the melin. Sometimes Nigel on his own, sometimes I on mine. When our time there coincided, it avoided friction such as the weekend when Nigel returned and described to me the site where some new tunnelling had started. From his excited account I was able to tell him that that was the exact area in which I had, on my last visit, planted a hundred daffodil bulbs. There were a few dodgy moments.

The tunnelling was necessitated by having to rediscover the channel of the watercourse after it had come by pipe from the millpond above and turned the wheel. The outlet into the Meloch was obvious once we had slashed down a bit of undergrowth, and so was the confluence with the Dee, but where, under the sizeable area euphemistically called the drive, was the tunnel? If only there remained some sort of plan of the former layout; but it could hardly have been anticipated when the conversion was begun that a modern miller would be the buyer, who proposed to grind not corn but electricity. It was fortunate that Nigel was never happier than when given a problem.

After a frustrating week or two of digging and delving, it was realized that mechanized aid would be needed, and Massey Ferguson arrived in force. By now the drive resembled the face of a slate mine, having been surfaced with slate chippings, and was indescribably muddy. We were there in early December, and the work carried on after dark very often, lit only by the exterior lights of the melin, which were scarcely adequate illumination. It was consequently a memorable moment when one of the fellows employed on the prospecting knocked on the door and, when I answered, said excitedly, 'Tell sir we've found it!' They were marvellous men. Totally involved and identified with the scheme, as chuffed as Nigel when things went well and as disconsolate as he when they didn't.

That Christmas we spent in Wales working in the melin by day but sleeping in the cottage, as it was still furnished. I had spent a long day in the autumn bargaining with the previous owner over the furniture and carpets and ended up having bought most of it at a reasonable price.

One night – I think it was the night before Christmas Eve – we had just returned to the cottage after a hard day next door doing some of the 'few finishing-off jobs' Nigel had earlier specified. I was starting to think about cooking some supper when I heard music. The radio was silent and I realized that it was coming from outside. I went to the window. Standing in a semi-circle round a lanthorn – yes, really – was a brass band, eight of them, playing away like mad. I ran to the door, and Nigel joined me. They finished 'Christians awake' and we begged them to come in and have a glass of wine and a mince pie with us. The leader hesitated and looked at the bandmaster, who said that they'd like to but after they'd played a request for us. I plumped for 'Hark the Herald Angels', which was duly performed, filling the chill night air with enchantment and the surprise of it all. It was like a joyous welcome to Wales.

Over the mince pies and wine we learned that the Bala

band had been formed many years before and had
faithful musicians and followers. One further surprise
that was that the bandmaster was not a Welshman.
When the previous one departed, there was no other
available locally and the job had to be advertised. The
present incumbent was a retired Yorkshire miner and
after many thanks and good wishes for the festive season
the ensemble played themselves out with a lively
rendering of 'Ilkley Moor'. It was a treasured experience.

After we moved up permanently, they continued to
come each Christmas for four or five years until one year
there was silence. We enquired and were told that they
had been disbanded. There wasn't enthusiasm from the
young people to join these days, and the dwindling
numbers had rendered it impossible to carry on. We
grieved greatly but were glad we had known it.

The next stage of our enterprise was to convert the
little stable at the end of the cottage into a turbine house.
The turbine itself was still being 'done up' at Nigel's
works, and there was much talk of something called the
alternator which was being shipped from Ceylon. Nigel
had been out there several times for the commissioning
of lights which he had designed, and I gathered that the
alternator was a piece of equipment redundant to their
present requirements.

'What does the alternator *do*?' I asked.

'It makes the electricity, of course,' said Nigel.

He could be quite maddening at times, but I had my
own concerns and had to leave it at that.

We had decided that, in order to defray at least some of
the escalating costs of Nigel's hydro-electrics, we must let
both houses to holiday-makers. At least, I had. Nigel
viewed the scheme with gloomy foreboding. Who on earth
would want a holiday in Wales if they had the slightest
knowledge of the climate? 'After all,' he said, 'we came for
the rainfall, which can hardly be a prime attraction on
holiday.' In fact, it made no difference. They came in
abundance; the reason being, I suspect, that there was so
much more to do than just lie on a beach, for which,

indeed, the first requirement is sun. We could supply sailing, wind-surfing, fishing and swimming in Bala Lake, endless glorious walking country, pony trekking, golf and tennis, and latterly the swift-flowing rivers have made Bala an internationally famous canoeing centre. Few of these activities, for keen participants, required particularly good weather.

I started attending auction sales both locally and in London and gradually got the melin into shape for letting. We realized that we needed a letting agent who would not only take the bookings but generally oversee the properties, plus a cleaner for the days on which they changed hands. Our builder suggested a lady whom he referred to as 'Barney', who lived in a nearby village and had holiday cottages of her own. We telephoned her and made an appointment for her to come and see what we had to offer.

Barney arrived promptly, and we were on our very best behaviour. We really needed her and were anxious to present ourselves and our properties in the best possible light. She was a large lady, dressed in a tweed suit, with a pleasingly direct manner. Upright, downright and forthright and above all efficient, we felt sure. Having thoroughly inspected the two houses and made various suggestions – such as, 'You must provide electric blankets for all beds in this climate' – to our great relief she took us on. She even knew of a cleaner she was sure would be able and willing.

Barney became, and still is, a great chum. Even after we moved up, we still begged her to carry on letting the cottage, and later we built another one, up the hill, on the site of a collapsed pigsty for which we had inherited planning permission. We were certain that, left to us, the places would get double-booked and lead to all kinds of tangles. She had her own yardstick by which she measured complaints as either trivial or needing attention. A loose leg on a dining-chair was dealt with immediately but a charge of two spiders in the bath was met with, 'Have you made a mistake in booking? *This* is the country.'

Among all our other irresistible attractions we had

advertised free fishing in the River Meloch and the millpond, and a prospective holiday-maker asked, over the telephone, what kind of fish were to be found there. Barney wasn't often stumped but she knew less than nothing about the sport.

'I told him, oh the usual kind, you know.'

'Like cod and haddock and kippers,' said Nigel.

'You *didn't*, Barney, did you?' I asked.

Barney changed the subject.

Every year, in late October, she would arrive with her annual accounts, and she and Nigel would settle down at the dining-table with a bottle of wine and go through them. Her method of accounting was unusual, but Nigel finally got the hang of it, and it was always exact. Except for one year when she lost a pound; I think she's only recently given up searching for it. We particularly liked one entry. It said: 'To removing one dead mouse from storage radiator – 50p.'

'I think the tax inspector is unlikely to query our expenses,' said Nigel. 'Nobody could have invented that.'

On our first meeting we had told Barney that we wanted to book the melin for ourselves for two weeks in June, and both it and the cottage for Christmas. We had unforgettable Christmases. The open plan made it possible to have a twelve-foot tree, and we were able to hang presents, quite heavy ones, without its collapsing.

The finishing-off jobs were taking longer than even I thought, but gradually both houses were furnished and fitted to a standard I wished I had met myself in holiday homes. Only one of Barney's suggestions was firmly turned down by Nigel. Television. 'Let them look at the fire,' he said. 'The pictures are better.' He changed his mind later. In bad weather it kept the children off the beds, which otherwise they were inclined to use as substitute trampolines.

The excavations were now complete, and the drive at least was rolled and tidy again, ready for the expected visitors.

In May our banishment began. It was hard, but we

badly needed the money the holiday lettings were
bringing us. Not that the preparations were halted. The
construction of the turbine house continued and the
large, fertile, though overgrown kitchen garden on a
raised, walled piece of land in front of the cottage,
between it and the river, was ploughed and early
potatoes were planted. All had now to be arranged long
distance but it seemed to work remarkably well.

Our neighbours the Williams at the farm were very
helpful. They had a key and saw in deliveries of this and
that – a couple of times, large van loads of furniture –
and gave willingly of their time. They made friends with
the families who stayed and who bought milk and eggs
from them, and they said more than once how good it was
to see the lights on across the river again. In relatively
unpopulated areas such as ours, the word 'neighbour' has
a meaning unknown in town.

We longed for late June and our two-week holiday.
When it arrived, Nigel hacked his way round the
millpond with a hand scythe and saw, clearing years of
unwanted growth and very nearly finishing the job. It
was very hot and I worried that he might be overdoing it,
but he seemed to be wonderfully adaptable, and the
sudden transmogrification from desk-bound boffin to
agricultural worker seemed to have no effect at all on his
physical well-being. I'd never seen him so happy.

I spent my time weeding, raking and sowing my
vegetable patch. The early potatoes were well up and
looking very healthy, I was happy to see. In the evenings
we trundled a wheelbarrow down to the banks of the Dee
and collected driftwood for the fire, because at 500 feet
above sea-level, even after roasting days, when the sun
went down it was cool enough to need it. Wooding, as it
was called, became a way of life. On trips into London
after we'd finally moved to Wales, I would raid skips and
bring back the booty on the car roof-rack. And yes, that
fireplace gave me as much pleasure always as I had
imagined it would on first sight.

We spent two summer holidays and three Christmases

at the melin before at last we were able to claim it for our own occupation. In April 1975, we abandoned London without regret, for our new life in the valleys.

'Wales' means 'valleys', as does Vallais in Switzerland and Wallis in Germany. It was easy to see why they go on so much about them. 'How green was my valley' takes on a new meaning when you see it. You drive along a narrow, twisting road half-way up a mountain of rocks and boulders, supporting nothing but scrub and heather plus a few of the tougher and more foolhardy breed of sheep, round a bend and then, suddenly, you look down and there is the valley, with its winding river, fertile fields, a village tucked away at one end, and a verdancy that knocks you for six with its lushness.

We had come not only to Wales but, according to the guide-books, to 'the heart of Welsh-speaking Wales'. Would we be understood? There was no danger. All spoke English, although some were more fluent than others. It was interesting that, although Welsh was widely spoken, it was less widely written. This was because Welsh was traditionally 'the language of the hearth', and not until fairly recently was written Welsh taught. Many farmers whose English was, on the whole, very limited, nevertheless filled in all the inevitable forms from the Ministry of Agriculture and Milk Marketing Board in English. Very few could cope with the writing of their language. Now, of course, it is taught in schools along with English – which most children don't speak until they start their education.

There was above our famous hearth, inserted into those massive stones, an inscription on a piece of slate that the previous owner had had placed there, I imagine with the aid of an English–Welsh dictionary, which can be fraught with pitfalls. He had meant it to read, 'The mill is not grinding tonight', no doubt considering it an apt motto for a winter evening by the fire. The reaction of the locals varied from an ill-concealed smirk to a barely suppressed guffaw. It appeared that by some quirk of Celtic syntax the inscription can mean, 'The miller is not grinding tonight.'

'Quite possibly true,' observed Nigel, 'but I feel not exactly what had been in mind.'

Our new neighbours were very polite. One day before we had moved up there I was at the melin for a few days with an actress friend from London when I announced my attendance at a jumble sale that afternoon. Jumble sales are my passion, and I was amazed to hear that my friend had never been to one. However, not one to miss a new experience, she agreed to come. I explained that we must lunch early and be in the queue at least fifteen minutes before the doors opened if we hoped for bargains.

It was pouring with rain. The sale was in the sports pavilion and there was a small porch at the entrance. When we arrived, it was filled by five women chattering away in Welsh. They kindly squashed up to let us into the shelter, whereupon all conversation ceased. We were strangers. I daren't look at my friend. I knew I couldn't last out fifteen minutes of such silence and that I, at least, would get a childish attack of nervous giggles. After about two minutes the ladies resumed talking, but this time in English. Apparently it is considered ill-bred in the extreme to speak Welsh in front of English people who don't understand it. If you want an example of perfect manners, that was undoubtedly it.

Many incomers, as the English immigrants are called, younger and more intrepid than I, are learning or have attempted to learn Welsh. I know without being told what a difficult language it is to pronounce with English oral equipment, but they also beat their brows in anguish wailing, 'Oh, the mutations.' For instance, take the word *'melin'* (which incidentally is not unlike the French word for mill – *moulin*): in certain situations, which I can't begin to understand, this becomes *felin*, the F being pronounced V. If you want the F sound, that's two Fs. See what I mean?

In London it was afternoon before the furniture van was fully loaded. The men were going to stay the night in Llangollen, thirty miles from their destination, and hoped to be with us around ten the next morning. After

having to make three attempts to turn the huge
pantechnicon into our lane, they finally succeeded. I
then, and only then, believed in our new address.

The next few weeks were the usual scurry of fitting and
fixturing. The first thing that Nigel got down to was, as I
expected, fixing up his hi-fi, and on our very first evening
that vast area reverberated with the great big beautiful
noise of '*Also sprach Zarathustra*', so I felt truly at home.

The kitchen was transformed with pine units cleverly
designed to be fixed to the walls so that one could have
them at the height best suited to whomever was to use
them, and then the dishwasher was installed. I'd never
owned one before and I adored it.

On the day we first saw the melin Nigel said, 'This is a
place about people.' I agreed. Then, almost in the same
breath and contemplating all that space, he added,
'You're not going to fill it up with furniture are you?' I
pointed out that people liked to have something to sit on
but promised that I'd leave him plenty of scope for
pacing, which was the way he did his thinking. Now he
was thinking about dishwashers.

'What one really needs,' he said, 'is to have two.' His
reasoning, as ever practical, was that it was a chore
having to empty the thing, and if one had a second, it
would be unnecessary. The finished one would act as a
cupboard, full of clean dishes and utensils, which would
also save on storage units. We never did in fact get
another, but the idea has remained in my mind as a good
one.

I got on with my kitchen garden. The theory, stated
firmly in most gardening manuals, that planting
potatoes the first year on neglected land helps to clean it
of weeds was erroneous – at least as far as ours was
concerned. We bought a rotivator. This is a great piece of
garden machinery but only if your land is already free of
perennial weeds such as dandelion, dock and, the worst
pest of all, creeping buttercup; if not, all it will do is to
chop them into little pieces, and where you had one when
you used it, you'll have a hundred or more next year.

Every bit of those chewed-up roots will develop into a flourishing new plant the following season. I have already commented on the fertility of the plot, and the weeds loved it. There was nothing for it but to attempt to dig them out by hand. Incidentally, it was the only part of the so-called garden that had any depth of soil at all; the rest was very sparsely covered. This fertility, according to Nigel, was due to the miller's no doubt having for years, when clearing the millpond of silt, put it straight on the land, nothing being more nutritious.

'That would be hard work without a tractor,' I said.

'Oh yes,' Nigel replied, 'but he wouldn't have done it himself. He'd have paid a small army of little boys a penny or two a day to run up and down the hill with buckets of the stuff.'

Oh little boys, where were you now? I could have done with a few. Never mind, they'd done a good job, and I had one plot of depth and richness on our otherwise bald mountain. Bald, that was, but for grass and brambles, which nevertheless produced some of the most luscious and well-flavoured blackberries I have ever tasted.

The rest of the garden – the terraced part – I upgraded slightly during our time there, but the main improvement came from following written instructions on what to plant on poor, acid soil. I knew nothing of growing before Melin Meloch, but when we left, it didn't look half bad. Nigel used to say, 'If you can read, you can cook,' and I would say the same of gardening. I know that the sages often give conflicting advice, that the shrub or bush that you are about to prune looks nothing like the diagram in your hand, and as for the picture on the seed packet – well, enough said, but you *do* learn from their experience and your own what will and won't do well in your particular spot and even, if it doesn't sound too fanciful, for your own particular temperament.

I learned that my soil was too heavy to grow decent carrots or beetroot and that parsnips always forked because, although the soil was deep and good, the amount of stones could be only marginally reduced at each forking over. There were always more lurking below, and this is no good for the production of root vegetables. However, the crops that failed seemed to be the ones that were cheapest to buy; French beans, mange-tout peas and Swiss chard would proliferate way beyond predictions on the packet.

On a sunny wall I grew tomatoes and found that they needn't be, after all, red bags of tasteless liquid but firm and sweet and tasting of – I could just remember it – tomatoes. Oh, the cleverness of me! There's a photograph of me sitting cross-legged in the drive proudly displaying my first bumper crop of onions which Nigel learned to string *à la français*. I thought I was the greatest. Nigel once remarked that if the meek do inherit the earth, I'll be lucky to get a window box! My jubilation those first few years was due to the fact that, since I had never grown anything before, any edibles would have been a miracle, let alone this bounty.

Friends were unbelieving. It won't last, they said. Her whole life was acting – she'll never settle down in the country. Well, she did. The reason being that she had found something as satisfying, if not more so. Also it was something new about which there was much to learn, and that was truly exciting.

And the people Nigel had spoken of came and sat on the chairs and helped us. They seemed to find the place as fascinating as we did, luckily. Colleagues of Nigel's helped with the waterworkings, and my friends got dug into the soil and helped whitewash, and one made most of our curtains, and they really seemed to enjoy it. But the evenings were sacrosanct: we all knocked off at six for a happy hour round the fire with our drinks in winter and on the sun terrace in the summer. Nigel or I, sometimes both, cooked, and even friends tackled it from time to time. I have never been known to turn down a volunteer for any project. After dinner we would gossip, play cards or perhaps walk along the Dee, idly picking up a piece of driftwood here and there along the way.

We so enjoyed having friends to stay and got to know

them so much better than in London. There one met at
each other's homes for dinner, one eye on the clock on the
way – cursing the traffic, having to watch the drinks as
one was driving and mustn't be too late as Nigel had to be
up early for work. But here it was so different. Being over
200 miles from town, I told them it was scarcely
worthwhile coming for less than three days – preferably
more; so they did.

It was interesting to observe how they arrived full of
animation and determined to be good and entertaining
guests and then to watch the slightly false vivacity fade
away as the melin had its usual effect. This usually
happened after lunch on the day following their arrival.
They relaxed and started doing their own things. One
would hear, 'I'm going blackberrying. Anyone want to
come?' or, 'I saw a fallen branch over the road this
morning. Want to give a hand to drag it in?' and, 'Where's
the mushroom basket? There are some in the field at the
back.' There developed a saying, 'If it's Tuesday *or*
Wednesday, it must be Melin Meloch.' Such was the
timelessness of our life there.

Meanwhile Nigel's installations were coming on apace.
The turbine had arrived from the works, and also the
alternator, which by now I had learned was merely
another name for a generator, though of a fancier kind as
it made AC whereas a generator made only DC. Cor!
Both pieces of equipment had obviously been rebuilt with
meticulous and loving care and shone with glossy new
paint of the dark green picked out with gold which I
always associate with the more impressive railway
engines. A sluice gate was installed up the hill where the
water that would create our power was diverted from the
Meloch into the millpond, and another at the other end of
the pond above the terraces at the back of Melin Cottage.
By raising or lowering these gates, one could control the
flow of water both into and out of the pond and thence
into the sluice, at the other end of which was the pipe
which fed the turbine in its house below. The sluice gates
also acted as a safety measure to guard against flooding

when the river was in spate. I was at last learning some
general principles.

By now the cottage lettings were in full swing. Starting
at Easter, the bookings would continue more or less
uninterrupted until after the autumn half-term at the
end of October. The change-over day from one occupancy
to the next was on a Saturday, when our admirable Jane
Jones arrived to clean and prepare it for the next lot.
Very occasionally she would come and tell me that it had
been left so immaculate that she'd had almost nothing to
do and instead would remove some of the dust in the
melin for us. On one of these days Nigel commented that
he had observed that grandma had accompanied the
family that week, so he wasn't surprised. I asked him
what bearing that had on the cleanliness of the cottage.

'Oh,' he said, 'I saw her. She obviously thoroughly
disapproved of holidays and spent all her time polishing
the plastic.'

I always looked hopefully for grandmas after that, and
I must say that this theory proved right time and time
again.

My memories of the tenants are hazy and episodic. The
abiding impression was how little trouble they were,
which greatly surprised Nigel. His dismal forebodings of
being continually disturbed by knocks on the door
requiring information and complaining were not
realized. Some lessees we hardly saw except when they
arrived to pick up their keys and left to return them. In
between they were too busy enjoying themselves on the
beach at Barmouth, or down by the lake or clambering up
Snowdon. Others we chatted with when we met them
around the grounds, and some became temporary friends
who asked us in for coffee or drinks, invitations which we
pleasurably returned. One or two families came back
several times, and we exchanged cards and news at
Christmas.

Nigel had a problem. He had an appalling memory for
faces, although he did remember cars. The problem arose
if our visitors had changed them between one trip and

the next, when he would be completely foxed. Often when a car drew up and an occupant approached to collect the keys he would hiss desperately to me, 'Is it "How nice to see you" or "How nice to see you again"?' I would hiss back that the former would cover either situation, whereupon he would advance with a broad smile.

Quite unfairly, it was the few who did cause a hiccup in the smooth turnover of the lettings that I remember best. Like the Dutch family who came for the half-term holiday in late February one year. On the Friday evening, their last night, I came downstairs after a bath and was on my way to the kitchen to get supper when, in glancing out of the windows at the front, it seemed that a dense fog had developed. A closer look and I realized that it was not fog but smoke, and very thick at that. I opened the front door, and the merest sniff – choking and sulphuric – told me that a chimney was on fire, and it wasn't ours. I called urgently to Nigel to go next door to see what was happening, as I was unsuitably dressed.

He was back quite soon and looking distinctly puzzled. Apparently the scene in the cottage was entirely normal, not to say cosy. Mum, dad and the three children were sitting round the fire, cracking nuts and watching TV and the atmosphere inside was as clear as a spring dawn – not a puff of smoke to be seen. Nigel asked what fuel they were using. They seemed surprised and told him that they had been burning their rubber boots. Nigel was baffled but, as the view from their window was now clearing, apologized for disturbing them and withdrew.

We sat long over the supper table pondering the incident. They were not short of logs and surely, if one wished to dispose of one's wellies, the dustbin was the simplest solution? We finally gave up, agreeing that it was perhaps an old Dutch ritual performed always on the last night of a holiday. Well, we'd heard of burning one's boats, but really!

Nothing further was said either to or by our guests, and they drove off the next day with many felicitations and expressions of gratitude.

Neither of us ever forgot the Dutch family van Spud either, although they were charming. They just had a problem. 'Van Spud' wasn't their real name, of course. We called them that because about half an hour after they moved in, the head of the household knocked and enquired of Nigel, 'Please, how do you cook potatoes?'

Nigel started to explain. 'Well,' he said, 'you can peel them and boil them or cut them up and fry them or ...'

Our new tenant cut him short. 'No, no,' he said, 'pray come with me.'

Nigel accompanied him to the cottage. The predicament turned out to be the cooker, at which his wife was staring blankly and with a certain nervousness. Nigel explained the workings of the hot plates and turned one on to demonstrate. Minheer Spud was still puzzled and asked, 'But where is flame?' He had never come across an electric cooker before, as in the Netherlands the cooking and heating are done by natural gas. He nevertheless adapted well to this new-fangled contraption and made the most excellent coffee on it, of which we drank many cups with him and his family during their visit.

By now the millpond had been lined with heavy-duty polythene to avoid leaks, and the installations in the turbine house were completed and ready for T-Day, as we called it in June 1976. In theory. 1976, it may be remembered, was the year of the great drought, and we had to wait a frustrating three months until there was rain in sufficient quantity and enough water in the river to try it out. This was not until mid-September, and Nigel, I and two of his colleagues foregathered in the turbine house for the big switch-on. I was in charge of what is known as the governor, which I felt might be an error, but I did exactly as I was told and all went well. There were tears of ecstasy all round. We should have had champagne. The old mill was grinding again.

From that moment Pollyanna had nothing on us: we always had something to be glad about. There was no lovelier place to be in fine weather, and we also rejoiced in the rain, because rain equalled kilowatts. Without

water-power we could never have afforded to heat the
place. For those of my readers who have a taste for figures,
we produced 7½ kilowatts when there was plenty of
water, which there usually was in our climate. It was
seldom in an average summer that we were unable to
supply at least our needs for hot water and cooking.

The latter was done on an old cooker which was based on
the storage principle. It was GEC's attempted answer to
the Aga, and to my knowledge there is only one other still
in existence, which is in the Science Museum in London. I
believe that it never really took off but it was ideal for use
with water-power. It took only half a kilowatt and was
permanently ready with a large rectangular hot plate
which was kept under a heavy, well-insulated lid unless in
use. If one needed a hotter oven, one simply flicked a
switch which directed some extra heat in a downwards
direction. We also had a modern electric one which ran off
the mains and which was known as 'The Pay Cooker',
whose use was frowned upon except in cases of drought
and when Nigel was making bread, for which the free oven
didn't, to be honest, get quite hot enough.

We had, to the uninitiated, a bewildering assortment of
electric sockets throughout the house. Friends kind
enough to offer to do the ironing or a bit of hoovering could
be alarmed by cries of, 'No, no! That's a pay socket. Put it
in the other one!'

Drought was not the only condition that created a
shortage of free power. Heavy and prolonged frosts could
reduce the normally steep and swift-flowing river to a
mere trickle. Those were the only times when we used a bit
of coal. With the underfloor heating at a bare minimum, it
gave out considerably more heat than wood, and I loathed
it. Any puff of smoke ejected was so foul-smelling com-
pared with the evocative aroma of a log fire. When I had
been away, I would swear, even if I were blind, I'd have
known I was home again the moment the door was opened,
from the smell of the wood-burning fire. This was the case
whether the fire was lit or not. It was the smell of Melin
Meloch.

We adopted a redundant sheepdog named Fly – sorry Ffly; 'redundant' because she was too deaf and too blind to be worked any more. A more loving and loved animal it would be hard to imagine. She went everywhere with us and could be fast asleep in the back of the car when we turned into our lane, whereupon she would sit up and start sniffing the air. She, I have no conception how, also knew we were home.

Still on the subject of pets, I mustn't forget Mrs. I found her under the millstone table outside the kitchen on a cold November evening. Nigel was in Japan for a conference, and she and I both needed a bit of company. She was also very hungry and was drinking from a muddy puddle. All I had were some trout in the freezer by courtesy of the millpond. We were pretty unsporting. We didn't fish in the accepted sense, which I've always thought was a ghoulish thing to do anyway. I mean, you know how it feels at the dentist when he puts an injection into the roof of your mouth? Well then, look at some of those three-pronged hooks used to catch fish. Someone once said, 'If fish could scream, there would be far fewer anglers.' Anyway, Nigel, who loved trout, used to drain the millpond from time to time to rid it of some of the accumulated silt and then just pick them up. So Mrs had a fish dinner and, you'll never guess, there she was next morning under the millstone table doing her Oliver Twist bit.

Naturally she took up residence, and by the time Nigel came back she was well established. She was a highly decorative and characterful cat. We were glad she had chosen us.

I have spoken of the feeling of timelessness at the melin. In many ways this was so, but we were, of course, also bound by the cycle of the seasons, which quickly developed an unchanging pattern. Christmases were wonderful and greatly looked forward to by us both, but they were also tiring, and in early January, when all danger of further jollity from New Year had receded, we took ourselves off for a couple of days. Our choice was invariably Lake Vrynwy Hotel, a large Gothic edifice in which it was easy to imagine all kinds of Agatha Christie-like goings-on, although we never actually encountered any. The hotel was high above the lake itself, with a fabulous view. The light over the water and on the folds of the mountains which formed the banks seemed to change almost by the minute and was an unending delight until nightfall.

Having completed our 'good for us' walk, we settled down by one of the two huge log fires with our paperbacks in the happy anticipation that tea would arrive promptly at four and would consist of improbably thinly cut home-made bread and butter and other bakings, whose smell had been pervading the lounge for some time with forecasts of gratifications to come. Later, after leisurely baths, we would go down to the bar for our aperitifs and continue reading or play cards until dinner, which was always excellent and ended with a savoury – an almost obsolete course, sadly. They also, I remember, served grapenuts for breakfast. Hedonism could go no further. The bar closed during dinner but a delightful custom prevailed which consisted of arranging all the bottles on a table in the hall below a notice inviting guests to help themselves and enter libations imbibed in the book provided. Such trust arose from the implied assumption that, 'Our guests are gentlemen.' As with the Bala band, we had caught the end of an era. It doesn't happen any more.

After we returned home it was time to order seeds for the coming year and get stuck into renovations of Melin Cottage. It was a job I loathed. An old building, unoccupied for months, festooned with gungy cobwebs and dust which, when removed, revealed our tenants' indiscretions of the past season. Chipped paint, flaking walls, loose handles and the annual bathroom problem. The bathroom, having been converted from the front parlour, was downstairs and backed onto a small room at the rear of the cottage in which we kept the hoover, other cleaning materials and spares of this and that, such as light bulbs and rolls of loo paper. This was kept locked from tenants who couldn't have used it anyway owing to the condition of the two inside walls, which were crumbling alarmingly.

Half-way down these walls, one of which backed onto the bathroom, slightly below waist-height there was a wide slate slab on which the pig used to be salted to preserve it through the winter. The trouble was that the salt had permeated the walls and penetrated through to the other side, where beads of moisture coming through the plaster accounted for the detachment of the wallpaper, which by this time was hanging loose in a depressing and derelict manner. No expert could tell me of a product to cure the problem. 'Once you get salt into a wall ...', they'd say and shrug hopelessly. At these times with, 'just me and my radio', as the old song has it, I developed a close, though one-sided relationship with Jimmy Young. We spent many hours alone together in that cottage.

It was then time to dig over the kitchen garden, although we now had help. Raymond, husband of Jane Jones, would come at the weekends and in summer some evenings as well. He was, apparently, tireless and very strong. He would trench the ground and dig in the cow dung which was kindly supplied by Mr Williams across the Meloch.

In no time, it seemed, the Easter holidays were with us, and with them the start of the visitor season. Jane would come and give the cottages – we built the second one in 1977 – a final clean and polish, and we would replace any damaged or soiled furniture or utensils.

Replacements such as furniture and curtains which I picked up in auction sales we kept in what we called the dry store. This was part of the big garage at the top of the drive by the road. It was an extraordinary construction – for a garage, that is – on two floors which Nigel said had been used to dry the corn. A portion of the top floor we'd completely sealed off with walls of polythene

sheeting, and a powerful dehumidifier had been
installed. There was no heating but, as Nigel pointed out,
it isn't cold that destroys – it's damp. So, in theory, all
should have kept in the same condition as when first
stored.

Then one day, when searching for a mattress, because I
had put one of ours from the melin into one of the
cottages, we were confronted with a problem we hadn't
anticipated. Mice. They had eaten their way into a trunk
of bedding which had to be thrown out in entirety. Not
only that but when we found the mattress we were
searching for, one corner had been completely eaten
away. I think that was the first time I uttered the words,
'Never mind. It's only for us', which subsequently became
yet another motto at Melin Meloch. The best of
everything always went to the tenants. We retrieved the
dented, cracked, chipped and broken and repaired what
we could and used it ourselves. The chair with the wobbly
leg, the dented saucepans, the knives with loose handles,
all were gathered up and restored if possible, mainly by
Nigel, who, when I produced new casualties almost
weekly as the season wore on, would sigh and say
patiently, 'Put it on my bench, darling.'

I developed what amounted almost to a fetish about
toasters. I couldn't pass one up at any jumble sale. Nigel,
who in any case really delighted in sows' ears which had
the faintest possibility of turning into even cotton purses,
beavered away with them for an hour or more before
unceremoniously dumping them in the dustbin and
banging down the lid. He would then enquire how much
I'd paid for the latest irreparable objects, and if it had
been 20p or less he'd say, with satisfaction, 'Well, at least
it had a decent plug', and the decent plug would go into
the decent plug box. Sometimes he got them going, and
usually when he did, his repairs would last for years.

From then on it was seeding and weeding. The only
time I took off was the last week of June and the first
week in July to watch Wimbledon – yes, we finally
bought a TV, and a coloured one to boot, which seemed

the height of posh. Nigel remarked gloomily that he
didn't suppose it would make the programmes any
better, but in a way it did. It was easier to see the ball
during that sacrosanct fortnight.

During this time I would stifle all feelings of guilt.
After all, everything was sown and the harvest was still
some weeks away, so I could afford a little time off.
However, unconsciously I must have been riddled with
remorse for so neglecting my duties. I remember a
horrifying dream I had during one Wimbledon wherein I
was sitting on top of a tall step-ladder half-way down the
garden in the umpire's position – not awarding points to
the thrusting vegetation below but conducting them with
a baton. They were changing their shape and form as I
did so, and some, the McEnroes of the plot, were
becoming very ugly indeed in their behaviour. I was
desperately trying to keep control but felt horribly
threatened. It sounds amusing, I know, but I awoke with
a pounding heart and sweating with fear.

After the finals it was time to pick the redcurrants and
raspberries, which was no one's favourite job, but the
consolation of the thought of summer puddings, not just
in summer but all the year round, goaded us on, because
if there exists a more ambrosial delight I don't know of it.

August was a very wicked month. Friends with
children and those in the teaching profession all wanted
to visit us then, in the school holiday time. Useless to tell
them to book early for the peak period: they came in
droves. Some arrived with tents or caravans. Both
cottages bursting with paying guests, ours just had to
take their chances and when all our beds were full to
bring sleeping-bags. At least there was room on the floor
of the gallery – which curtailed Nigel's 'pacing space'
somewhat but was counterbalanced by the advantage of
more than adequate free labour for harvesting.

Our friends would pick and pod the peas and beans,
and Nigel and I would complete the operation. He
blanched and I would chill and bag them and put them in
the freezer. It was an excellent system. We had moved

with one small freezer and had bought two more
mammoths – one of which was housed in the garage. This
was an exhausting but very happy and satisfying time.
All was safely gathered in and Mr and Mrs Squirrel
Nutkin's hoard was laid up for winter's sustenance. One
product I found did not freeze well. Runner beans. I tried
blanching and not blanching, cutting them every
whichway and freezing whole. No dice. They were flabby
and boring. They ended up in soup, as we wasted
nothing.

Well, a lot of things did – end up in soup, I mean. I still
see our long pine table groaning with food, a large oil
painting of Nigel's only respectable ancestor ('All the rest
were cattle-rustlers,' he said), one John Spottiswoode
Archbishop of St Andrews, gazing benignly down upon
us. I would dispute this claim, saying that no one could be
archbishop of a golf course, but Nigel showed me family
records to prove his point. Anyway, to return to the
harvest supper table: I would admonish the company to
eat up or, 'It'll all go in the soup.' It all did. Our lunchtime
potage was usually a treat. Only once did our guests
mutiny and that was when I served up pastry soup. I
didn't blame them. It was fairly disgusting. Ffly ate it,
but then she would eat anything but mushrooms and
there were seldom any of those up for grabs. In a good
year a gathering of twenty pounds would not be at all
unusual of the largest and most succulent imaginable.
The freezers sagged with them.

The autumn, for the first few years, brought our
greatest problem. 'Autumn Leaves' is a beautiful and
haunting song. The fall, identified for so long with a
sweet, sad nostalgia, a magnificence of gold and crimson
under startling blue skies, became for us a nightmare.
We hated it. The reason for this was that the fallen
leaves blocked our sluice and had to be removed
manually with a hay rake at least three times a day and
often at night as well.

The night shift was no trouble to me if Nigel was at
home, but he was just as likely to be thousands of miles

away, doing something with lighthouses. On these
occasions I would be awakened at night by a gurgling,
sucking noise reminiscent of a saliva ejector of
gargantuan size. But I knew that it was no massive
dental operation in progress but that the sluice itself was
blocked by leaves, that the water going into the pipe
which fed the turbine was at a minimum and that if I
didn't get up and deal with the problem the turbine
would shut down and the melin would be pretty cold in
the morning. So up I'd get, wellies on, anorak over
nightie, and stump up the steps which led to the sluice to
start work. And it *was* work. A hay rake full of wet,
rotting leaves can be very heavy, and it took around
twenty heavings as a rule to clear enough to stop the pipe
gasping for breath – or, rather, water. I would then
return to bed, setting the alarm for 7 a.m. for a repeat
performance.

Later we tried wire netting over the sluice and then
mesh screens which rested each side and after a heavy
snowfall collapsed into it, unable to bear the weight.
Nigel was in New Zealand. I had to summon Mr Williams
that time. I just wasn't strong enough to lift them out
myself. After that Nigel had some fine mesh screens
made to measure and bolted in, but the leaves soon
managed to block them too, so the labour resumed. This
leaf fall would continue for three or four months every
year and took much precious time from other projects.

It was then that a friend who was also a water-power
enthusiast suggested a compressor. This was duly
installed in the turbine house with an air line running up
the hill and was programmed to blow air under the
leaves every so often. This stirred them up and prevented
blockages. Later on, Nigel automated the system, so that
when the water level fell low enough, the compressor
would straight away go into action. So no more nocturnal
sorties. Autumn again became a glory of mists and
mellow fruitfulness etc.

And how fruitful it was – our valley. Apart from what
we had sown and grown ourselves, there was the bounty

of the fields and hedgerows. The mushrooms I have already mentioned but in addition and all for free were blackberries, elderberries, crab apples, bullaces (the original plum – rather like a damson but sweeter), hazelnuts (if we could outwit the squirrels and get in first), bilberries and sloes.

So October was now devoted to preserving this munificence. Jams, jellies and purées of all kinds, along with sauces, relishes and ketchups, were bottled or frozen; nothing was going to waste as far as I was concerned. It became an obsession and, looking back, I realize this and am not proud of it. Often I didn't get to bed until 2 a.m., so busy was I adding to the stores. I was trying to do, single-handed, what in previous days would have been accomplished only by several women in a family all working together. It was crazy, Nigel said, and he was right.

His contribution, apart from general cooking throughout the year (he had a small but excellent repertoire), was to make our bread, which he did each week unfailingly, and also the wine. It must be admitted that Château Meloch was a great deal better some years than others, and although it was often possible to be amused by its presumption, it was equally likely to be pronounced fit only for cooking – and on one occasion its only possible use was as a substitute for vinegar. But, I recalled, the word 'vinegar' was a corruption of the French *vinaigre*, meaning sour wine. It was good vinegar.

With all that activity accomplished, suddenly it was time to order the Christmas tree again, and another cycle was complete.

There were, of course, variations in the pattern of our year. Unexpected exigencies, alarms, excursions and celebrations occurred as in any other household. I still did some acting from time to time for short periods. A television play or four weeks away in repertory was OK, but I finally lost my agent when I turned down an interview for a job in June, 'because I'll be picking the gooseberries'. I couldn't blame him. I did several plays at

Cheltenham in that lovely wedding cake of a theatre in Regent Street, now sadly and mundanely called 'The Everyman'. There, as there was no performance on a Monday, I could get back to the melin on Sunday morning and not have to leave before Tuesday afternoon.

I had a natural ability to entirely forget the theatre when at home, and vice versa, which was extremely useful. I looked forward to these breaks in routine. To do my hair and my nails and to forget my role as head cook, bottle-washer, laundress and housekeeper for a while was refreshing, and each job increased my pleasure in the other. I feel more people could benefit from changes such as I was lucky enough to have in my life.

When I was a child, my family had a housekeeper of uncertain temper and Thurberesque character. I well remember hearing her stamping up the hall one afternoon shouting, 'I hate the bloody lot of you. I'm going to run away and be a lady gardener!' Well, I didn't hate anybody, but the change of running away to be a lady actress was every bit as good as a rest.

Nigel approved of these occasional excursions of mine. He appreciated women who had interests outside the home, and in any case had always loved theatre. A friend of mine who accompanied him to a play disputed this, but it was true. He loved theatre so much that he became very angry if it were bad.

During one of my absences our open grate was replaced by a wood-burning stove. That is the bald fact. Before this was done, at least three winters of argument had taken place. Nigel had loved it as much as I, but it wasn't 'efficient'. I had come to dread that word – not that I wasn't all in favour of efficiency generally but I did feel that there were times when other criteria applied. I won't go banging on about the open fireplace again, but to my mind that was certainly one of them. However, I could see his logic, which was that not only did it burn about three times as much wood as an enclosed stove but the draught from the chimney sucked up a considerable amount of the underfloor heating, and even though it cost us nothing, it was poor economics. It also created a circulating draught which could be faintly felt all around the fireplace area, coming to its peak on the back of the neck of the person unwise enough to be sitting on the right of the grate. We did supply shawls neatly folded on the back of that particular armchair as a defence, but nevertheless there were comments.

One particularly cold winter I gave in but stipulated that I mustn't be around when it happened. So the deed was done. When I came home from one of my theatrical capers, it was there – sitting in the hearth looking smug – and, I must admit, snug too. It was much warmer, and I kept my sorrow to myself.

By this time everything connected with the turbine was automated. When I turned on the dishwasher or washing machine, the power required was taken out of the underfloor heat and returned to it immediately the machines were switched off. To me, who on a good day just about understood that there was no danger of the water getting into the wiring system and fusing everything or worse, and was amazed that the record-player didn't run erratically, the whole set-up was a major miracle.

Although we always spoke of our 'free' power, the installation, the building of the turbine house and all the tunnelling had, in fact, cost quite a bit. While still in London I would wake in the night to find the bed devoid of Nigel, whom I would find in the kitchen, drinking tea and pacing the floor. The costs were escalating alarmingly but he felt that he was too far committed to stop.

Nevertheless, it was a worrying period, and for the first time in his life he occasionally resorted to taking one of my sleeping-tablets. One evening he asked for one with his coffee, which I gave him. The following morning he told me what a wonderful night's sleep it had given him and was fulsome in his praise of what he called his 'beautiful lady'. This wasn't me, I hasten to add, but the pill, which was based on belladonna. After he had left for

work I found it, unmolested, under his coffee cup. He was
very suggestible. Associated with this, I feel, was the fact
that he never suffered from jet-lag. He lived so much
within his own head that the times at which he ate and
slept were entirely arbitrary.

Anyway, somehow we managed the financial crises
and, having done so, every time electricity costs
increased, the broader were our smiles. Two occupiers
later the turbine is still doing its job and, I'm sure, with
proper maintenance it will continue doing it for the next
century.

In 1978 we married. This was in strict opposition to our
beliefs. We had nothing against it for others but, having
both had fairly disastrous marriages previously and
having lived together in reasonable harmony for so many
years, it went against the grain. The reason for breaking
our vows were pecuniary and made financial sense.
Anyway we had the brief ceremony in London to avoid all
possible scandal! Nigel had been summoned for jury duty
on the date fixed for the event but his excuse of a prior
engagement, whose nature he described, was accepted
and he was excused. I think he secretly always wondered
if it might have been more entertaining.

Another engagement he was hoping to be offered was
from Her Majesty – to be detained at her pleasure. This
was on account of the fact that not long after the big
switch-on of the water power there arose a scare which
threatened to ruffle the smooth surface of the millpond.
This was caused by the sudden interest of the water
authorities in privately owned schemes using water-
power which, owing to the abundance of steep-flowing
rivers in Wales, were proliferating at quite a rate. They
decided to invoke the Water Resources Act of 1963, which
stated that in order to abstract water from a river to
create power an annual licence would have to be
purchased. This would apply equally to abstraction for
private or commercial use.

Nigel's case, for which he was fully prepared to be
imprisoned if necessary, rested on four points:

1. That he was not abstracting water but merely utilizing it and returning to the river the same amount in improved condition, because contact with the turbine had aerated it, and it was better for the fish. (There were salmon in the Dee, involving extremely lucrative fishing rights. Sometimes there were salmon in the millpond too which had lost their way – but that's another story.)
2. That as miller, albeit milling electricity not corn, he was in possession of ancient rights to the use of water. I think even Nigel thought he was on dodgy ground here, but it was worth a try.
3. That the Act made a nonsense of the government's much-vaunted and widely advertised 'Save it' campaign.
4. That what the Act was in fact attempting to license was gravity.

Nigel having made his views clear by letter and having gained the support of the National Association of Water Power Users, no summons was issued.

'They realized what complete idiots they'd make of themselves,' said Nigel complacently.

The Falklands War affected Nigel deeply. When the islands were first invaded, he sent a telegram to Mrs Thatcher. As I remember, it went, 'Do not heed the siren voices of the appeasers but seek ye the enemy within.' Shortly afterwards the lady herself started using this latter phrase. I have often wondered ... He cared terribly and became very 'Rule Britannia' about it. I think he would have sent the task force to liberate a single British sheep if necessary. He argued, 'How would we like to be invaded by a foreign fascist dictator and compelled to speak Spanish and drive on the wrong side of the road?' He was riveted by the newsreels of the intrepid yompers shown every night on television. He would dearly have loved to be with them and greatly regretted that age precluded any such thing. His reason was, in its way, romantic, I think – it was: 'It's all chaps, you see, the armed forces – no civilians involved.'

When it was over, he offered any unlet weeks in our cottages free of charge to any serviceman and family who had been there. We met some nice people that way. A petty officer, his wife and three incredibly well-behaved children were first. He was from the *Sheffield* and was followed by an officer from the staff of the operations ship of Admiral Woodward, who was accompanied by his wife and little daughter. Nigel invited them all in for food and drink and listened spellbound to feats of derring-do, asking endless questions and reminding me slightly of the painting *The Boyhood of Raleigh*. Luckily they seemed to want, even need, to talk, so it wasn't necessary for me to try to head him onto other subjects as I had felt might possibly have been the case.

It would have seemed strange to those who had known Nigel in his early days as a conscientious objector to find him cheering the prime minister through the Falklands War. Inconsistent? Perhaps; but I've never seen any particular virtue in consistency, and it certainly made for variety.

Variety indeed was the theme of our lives at the melin. When we first bought it, Nigel had said, 'Well, at least we'll never be bored. There'll always be plenty to do!' This was spoken with a gleeful rubbing of the hands. He wasn't joking!

2 Changes

For fourteen years this life continued. Busy and happy – tiring certainly but a night's rest producing renewed energy and enthusiasm for the coming day. However – and it seemed to happen, or I became aware of it, quite suddenly – fatigue was setting in. That energy and enthusiasm didn't, alas, spring from a perpetual renewable source. The stairs seemed to be getting steeper and more numerous. Nigel's arrangement of the white slaves, as he called the domestic machines, positioned as they were on the first floor, entailed many journeys upstairs to inspect their progress. Was the washer finished or was it merely thinking? And the tumble dryer, was it still turning or was it the sound of the Meloch that was always with us? Nip up and see – I didn't want the clothes to lie there and crease. The trouble was the nipping was quite certainly taking more effort now. Nigel had reasoned that, as most washing originated where one divested oneself of one's dirty clothes and bed linen, i.e. the top floor, it was poor time-and-motion study to have the cleaning apparatus on the ground floor.

It seemed like a good idea at the time, but that time, I could feel, was running out, and I could see that in a very few years it would have run. The mending and making good, the painting, papering and patching of Melin Cottage each winter were jobs I approached with diminishing verve also, and the climbing in connection with the weeding and maintenance of the terraces were frankly becoming an enervating bore.

I thought it over very carefully before broaching the subject to Nigel. We were going to have to move. There was no desperate urgency, I said, but wheels should be put in motion. After all, the greatest disaster would be to delay the decision until we were too inert to do anything about it. This I had seen happen in the lives of others, resulting in the despairing situation of looking on hopelessly at all the work and tender loving care lavished on a place being relentlessly returned to rampaging nature, and unable to muster the physical strength and mental resolve to do anything about it. I was adamant that this wasn't going to happen to us.

Nigel was not pleased. Yes, that is an understatement. We talked for many weeks, and gradually he genuinely came to see my point of view and to agree that it made sense. We had achieved our object. We'd created our own power, fed ourselves and our many guests from our own soil, and the cottages were letting well. To have quit in failure would have been unthinkable but it was triumph all the way. Melin Meloch went on the market.

Prospective buyers came and went. Sometimes the turbine daunted them; sometimes, I suspect, the stairs but more often the size of the place. Well, there were three houses, three garages and 1⅓ acres, which, of course, was reflected in the price. Nigel became despondent but I didn't.

'One day,' I told him, 'someone will walk in and fall in love with it just the way we did.'

Nigel wasn't convinced. 'There aren't that many madmen about,' he said.

But I was right. After eighteen months it happened as I had foretold. One morning a man walked in clutching our details; we showed him round, he professed great enthusiasm and by early evening we had sold. The date for completion was agreed at three months ahead, and that was that.

So now where? Nigel felt he'd like to stay in the area,

and I, who always imagined I'd end my days in Brighton, yielded. In fact, we did go down there for a week to explore the possibilities, and I admitted that it wasn't what it was and that the rosy glow that still suffused me at the very name was probably nostalgia for my touring days, when it was the most prestigious of all the dates. A girl friend in the same show once remarked, 'I *always* pumice-stone my heels for Brighton.' That put it in a nutshell.

We would have liked to build, but planning permission in Snowdonia National Park was practically non-existent. The authorities had become very protective, and one hardly blamed them. We finally settled for a modern house in a village three miles away, where I am still living. I have forgone character for comfort, and I don't regret it.

Memories of Melin Meloch are numerous and vivid. It was so very much the right place at the right time. A time for sowing and for reaping, for plotting and planning, of the joy of friends, of warmth and love and the pleasures of achievement. In short, the realizing of a dream; one could ask no more.

In October 1986 Nigel seemed slightly down. Nothing one could pinpoint – just not quite himself. I put it down to a lingering melancholy and sense of impending loss at leaving the melin, even though by now he was in full agreement. He had had a long-lasting bout of influenza early in the year which antibiotics didn't alleviate, and the attack had weakened him somewhat. But he recovered after about five weeks, and I thought all was well again. In fact, it seemed so for several months. And then the pain started. It was in his shoulder blade and was promptly diagnosed as muscular. He was prescribed pain-killers and a bottle of embrocation and, when these proved useless, stronger pain-killers and various sprays.

Looking back at this time, Nigel was surprisingly patient, but he was worried that, if he didn't improve, he'd be unable to help with the move as almost any

movement of his right arm increased his suffering. Only
in bed could he find any ease, and he started to spend
most of his time there. Obviously something more must
be done. An appointment was made for him to see an
orthopaedic consultant who had a monthly clinic in Bala.
X-rays were taken, his condition was pronounced not
serious, and he was told to attend the next month if he
wasn't better.

After two weeks with no sign of improvement, a friend
told me of an excellent new rheumatologist who had just
come to work in Chester. I more or less demanded that
Nigel be referred to her. An early appointment was
arranged. We were both greatly taken with this lady,
who after much questioning gave Nigel a thorough
physical examination, and more X-rays were taken. She
told us that the best thing for him would be to have some
traction sessions three times a week at Wrexham
Hospital. This would entail a sixty-mile round trip for us,
but who cared if he could be freed of that perpetual pain
he had suffered for so long?

The following Sunday, having not yet received an
appointment card, I was certain, quite suddenly, that
Nigel's pain was not muscular. He spent his time in bed,
lying on his left side as it was the only position in which
the pain was slightly eased. He still liked to come down
for meals but often couldn't last out and would leave his
food and return. This happened on the Sunday in
question, and as I watched him climb the stairs, dragging
himself up by the banister, I saw that he was sweating
heavily. As soon as I had settled him down, I rang the
doctor. The younger partner was doing duty that
weekend. His wife answered and told me that he was out
on a call but she'd give him my message. My message was
unequivocal: 'This man is seriously ill.'

The GP appeared, and the news wasn't good. A note
had arrived at the surgery from the lady in Chester saying
that after careful study of the X-rays she thought that Mr
Spottiswoode's pain might be connected with a chest
problem. Two days later we were at Wrexham Hospital –

not for Nigel to undergo traction as anticipated but to see
the chest specialist and to be told that he had a fatal
disease. I felt that the news was broken to us in a very
inhumane manner, but perhaps there is no way to
sweeten the statement, and the sooner the news is
conveyed the better for both the giver and receiver. In
any case, I wouldn't want the job.

'You have an inoperable cancer of the right lung,' said
the great man, and he pointed to a large X-ray
photograph blown up on a screen in front of us. All I could
see, as usual, with my untrained eye, were blobs and
shadows. The consultant pointed to one of the blobs,
which appeared no more remarkable than any other.
'There, that's it,' he said. But curable surely? My mind
automatically shying away from a truth that I couldn't
accept. I mean, they've made such strides ...

We were sent to X-ray. Nigel was taken in and I
waited. The consultant joined me. I popped the question.

'He hasn't long to live,' was the answer.

'What do you mean by "not long"? Months, weeks?'

'Oh, months,' he answered, 'about five, six at the most.'

I can't explain what I felt. I don't know what I felt –
even now. The man was still talking. Saying that he had
a clinic the next day in Bala, and I could come to see him
there if I liked. I believe he wanted to be kind but I didn't
go. I didn't see what we'd have to talk about.

I cursed myself for not realizing what the trouble was.
Nigel had been a very heavy smoker but had given it up
eight years earlier, as had I.

I'd tried hard for many years to get him to stop, in the
face of informed professional opinion, but he had always
shrugged it off. 'Never trust an expert' was one of his
famous dinner-party conversation-stoppers – or sometimes starters. But the fact that, in the face of the
overpowering evidence against the addiction, he had
finally managed to give up all that time ago, combined
with the fact that the pain was in the shoulder blade and
not the chest, had contributed to putting me off the scent.

Nigel rejoined me, dressed, and we returned to the car.

I didn't turn the key. We sat staring at the rain streaming down the windscreen. It was two weeks before Christmas. At last Nigel spoke. 'This is extremely inconvenient,' he said. This reaction was typical of the man. He had the wriest, driest sense of humour I have ever encountered. Not long after we met, I remember telling him that in my opinion his only fault was that he was too predictable, that, although no doubt perverse, I enjoyed being kept guessing a bit more often. Nigel considered this for a few moments and then he said, 'Tell you what. In future I'll be unpredictable on Thursdays.' But I wasn't laughing this time.

We drove home. That evening – still numb – a new but already dear friend, Gabby, telephoned to hear the verdict. I told her and mouthed to Nigel who it was, and did he want to speak to her? He did, and I heard him say, 'Well, at least I lived long enough to meet you, love.' Speaking to me later she said, 'That really broke me up.' Me too.

The next day Nigel was calm and very pulled-together. He made appointments to see our solicitor that afternoon, and the bank manager the next. His affairs and will were in good order but there were odd points that he wanted to check. We received a call from the hospital, which had by this time received the results of the X-rays. They asked us to go back to see a doctor from the Christie Hospital in Manchester in two days time.

The Christie Hospital is one of the foremost cancer treatment hospitals in the country, and Nigel was admitted the day after Boxing Day and given four X-ray therapy treatments. These produced the most miraculous result. The pain, which was due to the pressure of the cancer on a nerve, was entirely relieved by the shrinking of the growth, to the extent at which it caused no further suffering.

Back home again, with Nigel free from pain, I tried to make everything as easy as possible for him. Nigel himself vacillated between belief in and total rejection of death, and busied himself with sorting out his desk and jettisoning surplus papers.

It was a day or two before I realized that his behaviour was becoming more than a little frenetic, to say the least. He would go up to his desk, work there shredding paper, come down and in no time rush up again to check on some figures and return bringing more paperwork with him. He'd write lengthy letters to his accountant, stockbroker, bank etc, most of which I tried to convince him were quite unnecessary to do at that moment – if indeed at all. I started keeping any post connected with finance away from him, and myself dealt with the usual household accounts such as the telephone and electricity, because even they sent him into a frenzy of checking and referring back to previous demands, an attitude completely alien to his normal temperament. He wanted to pay the TV licence, although it wasn't due until July, and sent off a post-dated cheque which, incidentally, was how I found out they don't accept them. (If there is a reason for this, I can't think of it.) Figures bothered him, and the fact that he had always found them easy bothered him still more. Wherever he went in the house, he carried reams of calculations and sometimes would get up in the middle of a meal because he suspected that his calculator was at fault.

He became very bitter and cursed the medical profession. I could hardly blame him here – at least his feelings; but even if, with an earlier and exact diagnosis he could have been spared a great deal of pain over a considerable period of time, I realize that nothing could have saved him. A five-year survival rate in lung cancer is still less than ten per cent. This particular cancer is so late to show its existence. But Nigel was disturbed and angry.

There came a day shortly afterwards when I could no longer ignore the fact that he was losing his mind. He had been awake nearly all the night with an attack of hiccups – something he had never been prone to. It was frightening and exhausting for him, and as early as I dared I telephoned the doctor, who came quickly and prescribed Largactil. This stopped the hiccups and calmed him down, and that night he slept for sixteen hours. The next morning, although he felt better, his hands were shaking so much that I refused to let him shave with a safety razor and told him that a friend was bringing his own electric shaver to lend him.

'What time is he coming?' Nigel asked. Around eleven, I told him. 'Well, in that case,' he replied, 'I shall certainly need some more piccolos and probably a couple of flutes!'

I thought he was joking but it was a far from laughing matter. That same day he not only thought we were in Denmark but decided that it was imperative to write three letters to his cousin Marianne in New York – simultaneously! He had three pieces of paper in front of him and was writing a line at a time on each – a different line on different aspects of his recent battle with lung cancer, which, however, he stated was now completely cured.

As the days went by, his behaviour and thoughts became more and more bizarre. He heard electrical impulses behind a large, old-fashioned enamelled flour bin on a high shelf in the kitchen and got out the step-ladder to investigate, bringing down the bin, which hit and broke a jar of clear honey in its descent; he ended up with a mixture of flour and honey all over himself, the fridge and the floor. On returning downstairs after a much-needed bath and shampoo, he was wearing his underpants outside his trousers, and an argument ensued as to the inappropriateness of this. I gave in – after all, we weren't going anywhere. He also insisted that I put a notice in the local paper in order to thank '... all friends, Welsh and English, for their kindness and support during his recent attack of lung cancer and was happy to report that he was now well on the way to recovery'. I stared helplessly at the announcement, written now in a very shaky hand, and did as he asked. It wasn't the time for normal feelings, such as embarrassment.

Clearly a brain scan was needed. Wrexham Hospital had only that month installed one, after years of jumble sales and coffee mornings on its behalf, and Nigel was among the first patients to (I nearly wrote 'benefit') be diagnosed by it. The result was not unexpected. The cancer had spread to his brain. This, I discovered, is common in lung cancer; in fact, quite often it is the first symptom to show itself – well before any pain or cough develops.

Our GP told me that a drug called Dexamethazone, although in no way a cure, would probably help Nigel's state of mind by reducing the pressure of the growth on his brain. However, he said that he himself could not prescribe it, and it would all depend on the Christie consultant's view the next time we saw him. With relief I realized that this was only a day or so away. I was taking no chances: I scribbled a note telling him what our doctor had said and begging him, if he saw fit, for the drug that promised the chance of an easier time for us both. This I handed to a nurse, asking her to give it to the doctor before he saw Nigel.

We waited, sitting on the long benches in the out-patients' waiting-room, Nigel staring straight ahead in what seemed an almost catatonic trance and ignoring any of my attempts at conversation. At length we were called to an ante-room, where he was told to strip to the waist and wait. He sat on the examination table in his underpants, and I noticed how desperately thin he was getting. I felt lost, lonely and helpless. The consultant came in. I whispered, 'Did you read my note?' He nodded and with professional cheerfulness addressed Nigel with, 'And how are you feeling today?'

Still staring into space, Nigel replied. 'I live in Bala,' he said, 'and my wife is out all the time.'

'What?' I said, utterly staggered by this statement.

Nigel turned his head to look at me for the first time and smiled in a kindly manner.

'Correction,' he said. 'My wife is out *most* of the time.'

I looked helplessly at the doctor. 'I never leave him,' I said. He nodded and wrote a prescription for Dexamethazone.

The result of this was remarkable. Within twenty-four hours of starting to take the drug he became very nearly himself again – his very nicest self, gentle, amusing and above all calm. Unfortunately there are side effects, and I gather the drug is given only when death is inevitable.

That Nigel was on an even keel again was a double comfort. With our moving day getting closer; it had been arranged that until the move was completed, he and the cats would go to stay with friends Gavin and Rita Miller, who lived near Dolgellau. They had for many years been letting cottages – although many more than we – and were just starting to think of selling up and living a quieter life. (It comes to all of us in time.) Their house was in one of the most beautiful imaginable positions above the Mawddach river valley and with truly panoramic views in all directions. They were deeply fond of Nigel and he of them. A similar relationship existed in the case of the cats and was equally important. To have inflicted upon them a guest displaying anti-social and eccentric behaviour could not have been considered. I had telephoned various nursing homes in the vicinity whose staff would, I thought, be more conversant with these vagaries of conduct, but they were all full up and I'd been starting to feel desperate. But, hosannas in the highest, all was now well.

The move itself could have been worse – but not much. However, everyone has experienced it, though not, I dearly hope, in the same circumstances. I had sold the contents of the cottages to the incoming purchaser, as well as several large pieces from the melin which would have been quite out of place in a modern house. Owing to the scale of the former, artefacts needed to be the size of pantomime props to appear remotely in proportion, and I had acquired them accordingly.

One such was one of those oval rattan wicker chairs which hung from a beam far above. It was planned to be permanently in position – replacing an armchair by the fire. In fact, it didn't work out as, when not controlled by a sitter, it would revolve slowly on its axis fourteen times one way and then reverse and repeat the exercise. It seemed to be competing in the age-old quest for the secret of perpetual motion and drove everyone bananas. One evening, quite late, when an old girl friend was staying, I was sitting cross-legged in my Oriental cradle feeling wise and Confucian when my friend could stand it no longer.

'I've had quite enough to drink,' she said, 'without you rotating like a top all night. I'm going cross-eyed.'

It was time to think again. Nigel bought a pulley, and the offending object was banished – hoisted skywards, where it hung immobile except when lowered, which became mainly for the amusement of visiting children who nevertheless were informed that any bad behaviour would be punished by hauling them up twenty-five feet into space and leaving them. A modern oubliette. Naturally we never carried out our threat – although greatly tempted by the kids who thought that actually it would be a great treat.

Nigel had arranged that his son-in-law (his daughter Caroline's husband), who was living and working in Denmark, and his nephew James from California would come over and help me with the move. Help they most certainly did. Sensible, practical and tireless, they got on well together and were beyond praise. Gabby, who, with her husband, was preparing to run a guest house and had quite enough to do at home, cooked and brought down to the new house a hearty and beautifully cooked meal each evening, and filthy and exhausted the three of us would wolf it down. Then around eight we would get cleaned up a bit and drive over to see Nigel, a forty-mile round trip. But just to see his face when we walked in was well worth it. He was avid for news of how it was all going, and regretting that he couldn't be part of it. He was happy with his friends but, even so, longing to see the new house again.

We managed to get the kitchen, sitting-room, dining-room and our bedroom in order before his return. The other two bedrooms were piled high with 'don't knows' and 'perhapses', and there I intended to leave them while I recovered.

Gavin drove Nigel back one snowy January day. He looked so frail as I watched Gavin help him out of the car, followed by the cat basket. There was already a cat flap in the back door, and having thoroughly inspected the house Deano and Pandy disappeared to explore outside. We had a couple of bottles of champagne to greet the travellers, and Gabby and her husband came in to help us with them and we all toasted Nigel's 'recovery'. Anyway, that's what he thought it was, which was all that mattered. He was delighted with all we'd done to make the house habitable in under a week and greatly enjoyed partying with friends. The boys and I agreed that it had all been so worthwhile.

James and John left with our undying gratitude, and Nigel and I enjoyed – if it doesn't sound too absurd – an idyllic week. But the following Sunday – it seemed to be always on Sunday – he experienced violent pains and was rushed into hospital. I had been told that the new drug had side-effects. Among them was a lack of warning of the pain of inflammation in other organs. It was acute peritonitis, and he was taken back to Wrexham hospital – this time, obviously, as an in-patient. Later he confessed to me that he had been feeling a certain unease in the region of the colon; when I asked him why on earth he hadn't told me, he answered, 'I'd never discuss my plumbing with ladies!'

He was operated on and survived – just, and in passing I must comment on the dedication and skill of the Indian surgeon and Sri Lankan woman anaesthetist who performed the operation. As it was a weekend, all the bigger-wig doctors were not on duty but, knowing of Nigel's condition and that he had only a short time to live, they brought him through. I gather that this is regarded as a controversial procedure in certain circles, but any criticism on the lines of wastage of resources on a dying man would have me to contend with. Enough to say that, after he had recovered from the operation and came

home, Nigel and I had forty-eight days together in which
he was serene, happy and free from pain, which I regard as
beyond price.

During Nigel's second period in hospital, in between the
times I spent there, I set about arranging his funeral.
Referring to the *Open Space* booklet (Section E, 'Doing it
Yourself'), I refreshed my memory. Richard Buckley, a
retired funeral director stated, 'Nothing says you must
have a funeral director to carry out a funeral – nothing
says you have to take a body to the crematorium in a
hearse. You can use an estate car. You can provide your
own bearers and naturally you can arrange for a minister.'
Nothing says you have to have one of these either. He goes
on: 'Any wholesale firm will provide you with a coffin as
long as you pay; they're not fussy who they provide.'
    Great, I thought.
    Armed with the yellow pages and a mug of coffee, I
settled down by the telephone. Coffin wholesalers or
manufacturers, forward please! Strangely, none was
listed. I tried undertakers and was instructed to 'see
Funeral Directors'. Yes, of course – how silly of me, they'd
gone up market now, and it was funeral directors' suppliers I needed. There were several listed. I dialled. I kept
on dialling – firms within a reasonable distance, but none
was prepared to do business with me. Apparently the sale
of one coffin, retail, was out of the question; they supplied
only the trade. My request, they implied, was at the least
questionable, not to say outrageous!
    This was a setback I'd not expected. There was nothing
for it now but to try the undertakers themselves. The
results were the same. Coffins were supplied as part of
their full service only. Again and again this phrase was
repeated. So: utter refusal, and refusal couched in terms of
the most unctuous, sanctimonious cant imaginable. I had
reached an impenetrable blockade. My fingers had not
merely done the walking but felt as though they'd run a
marathon. This was the moment at which I came near to
giving up.

I went to bed very depressed, but it seemed my subconscious had other ideas, because I woke with the remembrance of the Humanists. They had to have an organization, I thought, and perhaps they could help. Directory Enquiries told me that the British Humanist Association lived in Prince of Wales Terrace, in Kensington. I wrote asking if my information still applied or had some legal restrictions been imposed since the programme had been shown?

The answer came in a very few days and was as follows:

I am very sorry to hear that your husband is dying of cancer and we can at this stage only send you our best wishes and understanding. It remains factually correct that you can buy a coffin direct from the undertakers. They cannot insist that you only have their full service. It is for them to accept your instructions in this matter. Also there is no legal obstruction to you taking the coffin to the crematorium in a station wagon.

The letter ended by wishing me luck but adding the proviso, 'If you, having thought about the matter very deeply, are convinced you can emotionally handle the situation.' I *could*. It would have been defeat over what I now knew for certain was a perfectly reasonable and legal procedure which I would have found hard to handle.

In passing, I would like to say how grateful I was for this friendly and sympathetic, as well as informative, advice from the Humanist Association. It gave me the encouragement I needed to carry on trying.

After breakfast I started afresh. There were still a few funeral directors within a thirty-mile radius I had not, as yet, contacted. It was the same story with the first three but the fourth told me that I would be certain to get a coffin from a firm of suppliers in Birkenhead and was kind enough to give me their telephone number.

I dialled and this time decided to try a little subterfuge. I said I wanted it for an amateur production of James

Saunders *A Scent of Flowers* – a play I knew well and which required a coffin to be positioned downstage during the entire action.

A brisk, efficient-sounding female answered. I explained my requirement.

'Oh no, we couldn't possibly supply one of our coffins for that sort of thing!'

'Why not?'

'It might offend our customers,' came the prim answer.

I pointed out that, their firm being in Birkenhead and my production scheduled for one-night stands in village halls in North Wales, it would be unlikely that any customers for her wares would be among my audience.

'They are *all* potential customers,' came the sepulchral reply.

Afterwards I wondered if I had offered to paint the name of her firm on the coffin for all to see, it might have helped her business and consequently her attitude towards my custom. However, wry humour was not a quality I detected in the lady.

But back to our conversation. I tried to reason but succeeded only in further ruffling her feathers.

'Who told you that you could buy a coffin from us?' she demanded.

I told her; I could almost feel the bristles down the phone.

'Then why don't you buy yours where he buys his?'

'Well, where is that?' I asked.

'S. and S. Joinery, Stoke-on-Trent,' she snapped and down went the receiver.

Was this it? Directory Enquiries was ringing. Be still, my beating heart, as T. Wogan was wont to say. Hope was making my head spin. Cannot insist on full service. How far Stoke-on-Trent? No matter, I and my Metro would make it.

Number obtained. Dial again and the miracle happened. It was obviously an unusual request but the young gentleman didn't see why not. I asked the price of their cheapest coffin for cremation. These apparently

were made in veneered chipboard and would cost me
£24.50. What was the height of the deceased? I told him
Nigel's height and asked if the coffin would be supplied
with any kind of container or cover. No luck there but a
duvet and dustsheets would disguise the shape perfectly
well from the eyes of the squeamish.

I was asked when I would be collecting it. I wasn't sure,
I said, but soon, very soon; I'd phone and tell him within
the next couple of days. We bade each other a very
goodbye. I found that I was trembling. I could hardly
believe it. Oh, well,

> Patience and perseverance
> Made a Bishop of His Reverence,

I quoted out loud, light-headed with triumph as I opened
a tin of lunch before setting off on the thirty-mile drive to
the hospital.

The next day I was chatting to friends – Joy and Alan
Byrne. As with Gabby, we hadn't known them long –
almost unbelievably less than two years, but they
already seemed to be old friends. Like Nigel, Alan had
retired early, and they had enlarged and modernized –
quite beautifully – a cottage nearby which had been their
holiday home for many years. They had both been so
kind, caring and helpful during the whole of Nigel's
illness – staying with him so that I could get out to shop
and have a break, taking him to his hospital
appointments because their car was bigger and therefore
more comfortable for him, and in dozens of other, smaller
but no less important ways. It's not easy to find words for
what the two of them meant to me at that time. I just
remember the all-pervading feeling of reassurance that
they gave me throughout. I suppose I would have
managed to get through without them, but it's hard to
imagine how.

On that morning I was giving them the latest news of
Nigel. I told them of my plans – a little hesitantly, I
admit, as they are practising Christians and I wasn't

sure how they would take to the idea of a DIY funeral.
Their reaction was immediate, surprising and heart-
warming to say the least. It was that in no way was I
going to bring a coffin from Stoke-on-Trent to Llandderfel
on the roof-rack of a Metro and that they were driving
north for the weekend and would stop off and pick it up
on the way home.

Then started the discussion about where to store it
until the inevitable happened, during the course of which
the doorbell rang and an elderly neighbour was revealed
who had kindly called to introduce himself and to ask if
there was anything he could do to help me, as he had
heard my husband was ill in hospital. I was compelled to
ask him in, although it could have scarcely been less
convenient. However, he already knew Joy and Alan, and
the kettle was boiling, so I asked him to sit down, and
would he like to join us in a coffin? It came out so
matter-of-factly that even Joy and Alan didn't notice and
our new guest was, luckily, slightly deaf. I wished I could
have told Nigel: he would have loved it.

Eventually the three of us were alone again, and I
remembered that I had a large loft. The fact of the recent
move plus my mind's having been engaged elsewhere
might, I hoped, explain this otherwise crass stupidity.
The loft covered an area the size of the house, with
unused and shadowy places under the eaves which were
unlikely to be investigated – particularly by Nigel, who,
sadly, even if he came out of hospital would nevermore be
able to climb the ladder.

Alan checked by telephone and arranged to collect the
coffin the next Monday afternoon. Regretfully, the young
gentleman told him that he had quoted me the price to
the trade, and for a retail sale it would be slightly more
expensive, i.e. £36 plus VAT. All this agreed, there was
nothing more to do until it arrived. On Monday evening
Alan telephoned. They and the coffin were safely back –
the coffin in the Volvo, its outline well disguised by an old
car cover, and he would bring it round after dark the next
evening.

Come the following night, I was sitting at home with
Caroline (Nigel's daughter by his first marriage, the wife
of the 'moving' John, who had not long returned to
Denmark). She was in Wales for the second time that
year. The first time was in February, when she spent ten
days with us when her father came home after his X-ray
therapy treatment. This time she had been sent for
urgently because Nigel had taken a turn for the worse –
in fact, had nearly died after his peritonitis operation. We
had both spent three days and nights at the hospital the
previous week.

People are forever knocking the National Health
Service – I admit I am not myself guiltless in this – but
we couldn't have been treated with more consideration.
We were given a room with a wash basin and which had a
shower next door. Admittedly there was only a single bed
but that was fine by us; we kept it warm for each other as
we were doing shifts of two hours each. I insisted on
taking the two till four in the morning watch, as I had
read somewhere that this is the time when one is at one's
lowest ebb, and therefore when death is most likely to
occur.

During this time I noticed a definite regression in his
mental state. He would become irate and irrational,
shouting at Caroline and me and from time to time even
at the nurses, who were patient and sweet and had done
nothing to deserve it. After three such days the night
nurse told us she thought that Caroline and I were
exciting him and that it would be better if we went home
and merely visited during the day. I agreed, so long as
the houseman would assure me that he was out of
immediate danger. This was confirmed the following
morning, and that evening, not devoid of relief, we went
back to our own beds.

The next day, on our arrival back at the hospital, there
were bars up on the sides of Nigel's bed. He had
apparently been very obstreperous during the night –
trying to get up, demanding to go home and so disturbing
the other patients that he had been moved, temporarily

Nigel in 1984

The author

Melin Meloch from the mushroom field

The kitchen in Melin Cottage

The cottage sitting-room

The first floor gallery with hanging chair hoisted aloft

It's working!
Nigel and I in
the turbine
house after the
big switch on

The ground floor

Melin Cottage

The turbine house, Melin Cottage and the melin

to a private ward. So much for our exciting him, I thought. I had queried his dose of Dexamethazone with a nurse earlier, and she assured me he was getting it in his drip, but I have a suspicion that it had been reduced or even forgotten. They were all extremely busy. When he came home and I was able again to administer the tablets, he returned to normal. He even said once of that period, 'I was quite mad, wasn't I?'

As we heard the Volvo backing up to the house, Caroline jumped up and said, 'This is nothing to do with you, Jane. I'll help Alan up to the loft with it.' I felt my eyes filling. What a splendid person she was. I wondered if I'd ever appreciated her properly before.

The coffin stowed away in the loft and discreetly covered so as not to alarm the plumber, we all had a coffee with a small touch of something stronger, and Alan recounted how he and Joy had arrived to collect it.

'In this back street,' he said, 'they were making coffins like they were going out of fashion.'

I remember thinking that I wished they would. With the number of trees lost in the gales of autumn 1987 and again in 1990, surely we can devise some material other than timber products, to end up burnt or rotting in the earth? Later a sketch of a reusable coffin was sent to me by an interested correspondent. Primitive in design, maybe, but greatly advanced in thought.

This practical idea was put to a local crematorium by Diana Davidson, manager of the Citizens' Advice Bureau in Chichester. She said that she had had people come to her office in tears, not knowing how they could possibly meet the cost of a funeral. In the Chichester area, she said, the minimum cost of a hardwood coffin is £300, which, 'seems a lot of money to be burned'. Ms Davidson suggested to the crematorium manager that they might use a wooden coffin with a hole in the bottom. 'So,' she explained, 'the body could drop through and the coffin could be used again.' She added that such a design would cut costs considerably.

The manager was shocked. 'Oh no,' he said, 'people

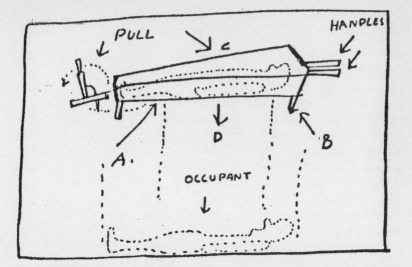

Sketch of a reusable coffin from a short story by
Ludwig Bemelmans published during the Second
World War. His text explains: ' "And with this
funeral goes a rented coffin – it saves you buying
one." A working drawing of this imaginative,
melancholy piece of black carpentry was attached,
also photographs showing its economical performance. It looked like any other frugal coffin, but had
an ingenious device – two doors at the bottom
opened when a lever was pulled. Once occupied and
having been carried to its destination, the coffin
opened at the bottom and the occupant was dropped
into the grave. So the rented coffin could be used
over and over again.'

wouldn't like that!' One would like to know how that
conclusion was reached. Had he taken a poll? If not,
perhaps he should before making such presumptuous
statements.

There are occasional glimmers of enlightenment
filtering through the more hidebound attitudes. At a
recent trade exhibition staged in Paris, a Spanish firm
was featuring a new idea in coffin materials made from
moulding reconstituted wood pulp from agricultural
waste. They are looking for partners to develop the idea
throughout Europe. One hopes they come forward in

sufficient numbers to make such an item available to all ecologically minded funeral-arrangers before too long.

Nigel really was a fighter. Shortly after all this, he was out of hospital and home again, convinced he had beaten his cancer and with a most positive attitude towards recovery. Due to modern miracle drugs, he was positively euphoric. We talked of all we would do when he was strong enough, and I put everything else out of mind and concentrated on being positive and cheerful myself, which was not always easy but I was determined to behave normally and to treat him as a convalescent and not as a sick man. It was not too difficult. Nigel had been very healthy all his life and, apart from a slipped disc and the odd bout of 'flu, had never been incapacitated for more than a day or so. He once said that he was not at all fit but was terribly well. This distinction was made after two of his friends who were really into fitness dropped dead — one on a tennis court and another in a gymnasium. However, he did know that he nearly died at the time of his peritonitis operation, and so it was easy to convince him that it would take quite a time before he was really strong again. He had indeed gained strength since he came home but was nevertheless prone to stumble and even fall, as the drug which was keeping his mind rational was also weakening his muscles and bones.

I felt guilty every time I gave him his tablets, and discussed it with our GP. The outcome was a decision to continue with the same dosage, because what is the use of physical strength without the brain to direct it? For example, Nigel had started to do a little cooking again, and there's no point trying to prepare a dish without the wit to understand the recipe when one needs it. (This indeed was starting to happen before he was prescribed Dexamethazone, and the results were less than appetizing.)

On 4 May 1987 a bank holiday Monday, we had just settled down to lunch before watching *A Man for all*

Seasons. Nigel had never seen the film and, as it was shown rather late, we had recorded it and intended to watch it that afternoon. We were discussing the order of Henry VIII's wives when suddenly Nigel started to make extraordinary labial noises, like a baby. I was about to say 'Stop mucking about' when he fell forward into his soup bowl, unconscious. I was terrified – both of leaving him and also of not leaving him, in order to go for help. Luckily he was sitting in a grandfather chair with sturdy arms which would prevent his falling, so I removed the soup bowl, turned his head on one side and rushed out of the front door, picking up our 'frog horn' on the way. (A frog horn is a gas-powered small-craft warning which was used at the melin to get Nigel down from the millpond to the telephone. It was purchased because the sound of the river made reaching him by any other means quite impossible. Car horns had no effect, and we were beginning to think that shanks' pony was the only way of attracting his attention when someone came up with this idea.)

I went out into the drive and blew up my horn like mad. The neighbours came to their kitchen windows better to see the antics of this strange lady, and I managed to yell, 'Get Trudie, quick!' (Trudie being Miss Prescott, who had just, with her partner opened a residential home a couple of hundred yards away, and is a nurse.) She was with me in no time, and while she and a neighbour carried Nigel to his bed, I phoned the doctor, who arrived very soon.

Nigel had had a brain haemorrhage. He didn't know the doctor and was very disorientated and frightened for the rest of that day and the next; but on the following one it was as if it had never happened. I'd told him that he had fainted, which he found fascinating. He continued to ask visitors for quite a while about their fainting habits. I told him he was lucky to be where he was when it happened, as when I first fainted it was in the middle of Watford High Street!

The doctor had told me that it was probable that he

would die from either an infection or a brain
haemorrhage. I had been repelling all visitors with even
the slightest suggestion of a cold but had no power over
the internal workings of his cancer. Anyway, that one
didn't arrive stamped 'fatal', and the speed of his
recovery seemed almost incredible.

Eventually, though, I could no longer manage him at
home – he was so weak; so I arranged for him to go into
the residential home, where Miss Prescott and Mrs
Whitaker did everything they possibly could to make him
happy and comfortable – and succeeded. It was, in the
circumstances, an ideal situation. His room overlooked
our house, and he could watch the comings and goings –
we were having some turf laid at the time in which he
was taking a great interest – and I used to drive round
there every evening at half past five and bring him home
for a meal, after which we would chat or watch television.

Sometimes he would last out until the end of
Newsnight, and other nights it would be earlier when he
said, 'I think I'd better go home now.' The fact that he
was already at home never hurt or worried me. It meant
he was happy in his room at Tirionfa, as it is called, and
in any case 'home', to Nigel, was always where his bed
was. Whatever time I ran him back, there was always a
smiling, cheerful member of staff to greet him, strap him
into the stair lift, help him to undress if necessary and
even bring him a last cup of tea if he felt like one.

During our evenings together we would talk about all
we were going to do when he was better and were even
planning a trip to North Devon to stay with our friends
Steve and Iris Pugh. I said we'd better take two days over
the trip and make a stop-over on the way. Indeed, it
didn't seem quite impossible even to me, as he seemed to
have reached a kind of plateau – no better but certainly
no worse, free of pain and very happy – often informing
me that he was getting stronger every day.

One evening he said he'd like me to fetch him the
following morning, as he wanted to make some bread.
This I did around eleven. He no longer made

conventional bread with all the kneading and rising stages, but soda bread, which is a simpler and much quicker process. When it was in the oven, I asked him if he'd like me to clean up, wash the pastry board etc, and for the first time he let me. Usually it was, 'No, thank you, darling – I can manage.'

After he'd taken out the bread, I took him back for lunch and he rested as usual in the afternoon, lying on his bed and listening to the radio. About five that afternoon Miss Prescott arrived with him in her car. It seemed he had become confused over the time I'd said I'd pick him up, although it was always the same, and Miss Prescott thought he was a little agitated and so brought him round herself. She also brought two double-sided tapes of *Phantom of the Opera* for us to play. This was one of the shows that was most definitely included in our plans to see, 'when I am better'.

Our friend Gabby was bringing round our meal that night. She phoned to say that, having only just returned from Chester, it would be around nine before she could get over with it, and would that be all right? I said, 'Fine,' as we were going to listen to *Phantom* and that would just about give us time. We listened and loved it, and Gabby arrived with her usual deliciousnesses and stayed and had a glass of wine with us as we ate it. It was a lovely evening. Gabby was at her most amusing and we laughed a lot. About eleven I noticed that Nigel had dozed off with a smile still on his face.

Next morning I had a call from Tirionfa. Nigel wasn't very well and was asking for me. 'No; no mad rush,' I was told, but Miss Prescott had sent for the doctor. I dragged on some clothes and ran over.

'I'm all right, darling – quite all right,' he told me. I asked if he wanted a drink. 'Perhaps a cup of tea,' he said.

The doctor came. 'He's quite poorly,' he told me, 'but knowing Nigel ...' He shrugged and spread his hands. I knew what he meant. Having survived peritonitis and a brain haemorrhage on top of an inoperable cancer, who was to speculate?

The doctor came three more times that day. Morphia was injected and oxygen arrived. I rang Joy and Alan, who came immediately and stayed, apart from a quick lunch break, all day. Nigel seemed quite happy, dozed a lot and knew that the three of us were there with him. Once he suddenly opened his eyes and said, 'Isn't everything lovely?' Huskily I agreed and smiled. So did he. Nigel was wont to say, 'Before knocking the iniquities of present-day science and talking about the good old days, think about dentistry, and modern pain-killing drugs and anaesthetics.' I *was*.

Around five o'clock I dashed back to feed the cats and to see the electrician who had arrived to fit a new ceramic hob which Nigel had ordered. All this took about four minutes. As I returned, I heard him say to Joy, 'I'm dying! *I'm* dying!' This was said without fear but with considerable surprise, as most certainly such a thought had not crossed his mind for months. He didn't speak again and shortly afterwards became unconscious.

Joy, Alan and I stayed with him, and Miss Prescott left his side only to get us coffee and sandwiches, and later scotch and sandwiches, as we waited. The doctor came for the last time and said, 'Yes, he's going now.' His breathing became more and more laboured, but I was assured that he was feeling no discomfort.

Nigel died at 7.30. It was 21 May 1987. In the end it was that valiant heart that gave in. 'It had had enough thrown at it,' said the GP. He'd gone without pain and surrounded by love. I hope that I may be so lucky.

Leaving Joy to help Miss Prescott with what are called the last offices (Joy is also a trained nurse), Alan and I went back to the house and between us brought the coffin down from the loft. He then telephoned Nigel's relations for me, for which I was most grateful – it had been a long day. He then proceeded, at the same time as refilling my glass rather regularly, to produce all the necessary forms which, bless his heart, he had already collected, for me to fill in and sign in order to have the cremation. This, according to Nigel's will, was to be done as quickly and cheaply as possible. Alan had also arranged that he would take Nigel's body to the chapel of rest at the crematorium until the cremation could take place. He then went back to Nigel's room to see how the women were getting on – and met the first snag in the arrangements.

There was no way that Nigel, in his coffin and with the coffin in a horizontal position, could be carried out of the room and around all the corners and down the stairs to where the Volvo was waiting. Perhaps the professionals could have done it, I thought, but we couldn't. (Since then I have learned that the way it is done is in a body bag, which is much easier to handle, and then transferred to a coffin either in the pick-up vehicle or at the undertakers.)

Joy and Alan came back, and it was decided that we would wait until dark and then bring him down the fire escape; luckily there was one right next to his room. Joy told me to find some sort of a lining, and off they went. I put an old eiderdown and a small pillow in the coffin and waited.

In five minutes or so they were back. Nigel was strapped into a light commode in a sitting position and had been carefully carried down the fire escape to the waiting car. (I learned from this experience that rigor mortis takes much longer to set in than I had supposed; quite some time, in fact.) Thus Nigel, in the Volvo, came home. We laid him in his coffin on the spare-room bed.

I was glad it was all over for him – and, it must be admitted, for me too. Knowing that he was unquestionably going to die, and not knowing how or when, had been a strain, and the fact that it had been so much easier for him than might have been the case was a great relief. He looked serene – I know that is always said about the dead, and after all, how else would they look? But nevertheless, that was a comfort too. In reflecting on the day, after Joy and Alan had gone home, I was surprised that it had seemed so unfrightening. Being 'in on it', so to speak, had dissolved fear; and death, for the first time, seemed as natural to me as birth.

I made myself a coffee and went to bed, pausing to look in and say goodnight to Nigel on the way, which at the time, and since, didn't seem at all an unusual thing to do. Much later it struck me as odd that I experienced no superstitious fear or repugnance in the presence of a dead body, although I am so squeamish that more than once I have had to ask a neighbour to deal with a dead rabbit that one of the cats had brought in during the night.

I slept soundly, a good thing in view of what the day was to bring. On waking I had a look at Nigel and then telephoned Alan, to find out when he would be ready to drive him to the crematorium mortuary. Alan had been busy and had arranged the cremation for the following Wednesday morning. The unusual delay was because Nigel had died on the Thursday before a bank holiday weekend, but as soon as our GP had signed the death certificate he would be on his way.

Then began a day of great anxiety, to put it mildly. On telephoning the surgery, I discovered that before a cremation can take place the death certificate has to be signed by two doctors – one of whom must come from outside the area. The dilemma arose because the doctor coming from outside the area could not get there until 6.30, and the crematorium mortuary closed at 4.30 and didn't reopen until the following Tuesday. Another setback. I had known, of course, that the signatures of two doctors were necessary for certifying the insane, and found myself saying, 'But he's not mad. He's only dead!' But there was no bending the law, even though Nigel had been 'under the doctor, on tablets', as they say around here, for many months. I realized the reason, of course. A cremated body cannot be exhumed should there be any suspected need for re-examination at a later date.

I phoned Alan and explained the problem. He said he'd phone me back. At that time I didn't pause to wonder if he'd realized exactly what he'd taken on when he first became involved with Nigel's funeral arrangements; I did later, and often, with deep and loving gratitude. After a short time he called back. He'd found out that there was a

public mortuary in Bala and to get on to my GP about it.
So back to the surgery. The ladies in reception knew of no
such thing. 'Please ask the doctors,' I said. The answer
came back: 'Not to their knowledge!' I put the phone
down. I was practically screaming with frustration. It
rang again almost immediately – Alan again, asking if I'd
had any luck. He said that there was definitely a
mortuary in Bala and had been told that the key was
kept at the police station.

The police, most of whom I knew, because of the great
help they had given us when we had been burgled a
couple of years earlier, said no, they didn't have the key,
and in any case it was the council who must be
approached. The sergeant offered to phone Mr Jones for
me, and told me to stay around because Mr Jones would
no doubt ring me back.

There followed what must have been the longest two
hours of my life. I paced the house for an hour or so and
then got on to the council office. Mr Jones was out but
would most certainly be in touch when he came back, and
yes, the police had phoned and Mr Jones would be given
the message as soon as he came in. I waited.

Alan phoned again. Neither of us spoke of what failure
would mean. Obviously it was not a good idea to keep
Nigel at home for what was little short of a week.

Around lunchtime Mr Jones was on the line. 'Hm! You
have a problem,' he said and (blessings on him always)
said he thought he could help. The mortuary was a
one-slab affair, intended, I think, for coroners' cases and
situated in the large council car-park next to the public
conveniences. (Incidentally, this building was a stone's
throw from the doctor's surgery and within sight of the
door.) Mr Jones didn't have the key; it was kept at the
ambulance station, whose staff would be told to lend it for
the purpose required.

I put down the receiver and wept. I realized that I had
a splitting headache and that my knee joints were
uncertain of their purpose when I stood up. But the glow
of achievement soon cured all that.

Much later I recited the story of 'my day in search of a morgue' to a friend who runs a residential home on the south coast. I asked her what on earth happens to people who don't live in a small town where they are known and therefore helped. She replied, laconically, 'The undertakers deal with all that.'

'Not any more,' I said. 'I'm starting a new trend!'

'You'd better not,' she replied. 'Many of my best friends are undertakers!'

I supposed that they *would* be, in her job!

It was quickly arranged that Alan would come at two and, with another friend, Dei Roberts, would take Nigel to the car-park mortuary. Alan and I put the lid on the coffin and screwed it down. I was touched to see that Dei had changed from his working overalls for the operation, although he would have to change straight back again after completing it.

So Nigel was leaving home at last. Combined with my relief that a resting-place had finally been found was satisfaction that I'd had him with me for those first few hours and that he had not been whisked from his bed by complete strangers and reappeared, repackaged, at the crematorium a week later.

Back in the spare room there were problems. It had just been decided that it was not possible that the coffin in a horizontal position could be manoeuvred around the many angles of doors and walls between there and the front door. The window was not wide and was fitted with secondary double glazing. After a heart-stopping few minutes it was realized that it could be just squeezed through with about three-quarters of an inch to spare.

Now the difficulties were almost overcome. It wasn't easy to get Nigel out of the window – and the large oval bed of rose bushes with the most vicious imaginable thorns, immediately underneath the window, didn't help – but eventually he was again steered into the back of the Volvo, and Alan drove off with Dei at his side. I followed in the Metro.

Once in the car-park I waited while the men unloaded

the coffin. We didn't have to stop at the ambulance station for the key because Dei already had it – one of the ambulance drivers being a cousin of his. (Everyone is someone's cousin in Bala, and a great help it has been on several occasions.) While I was waiting in the car (I thought the men would only be a few moments), Alan suddenly appeared at the window. He had left the Phillips screwdriver in the spare room after we'd put the lid on. There was nothing for it but for me to drive the ten miles there and back and pick it up, because the doctors would need to examine him and sign the certificate at 6.30. Before setting off I had a thought that just possibly there might be such a tool at the surgery that would save me the extra journey. There wasn't, but at least I was able to supply the information that there was indeed a mortuary in Bala and, 'Look, there it is.' The reply, which has mystified me until this day, was, 'Oh! we didn't know you meant *that* one!'

So back to the house, screwdriver delivered to surgery, and home yet again. I slept and slept and slept! Gabby and her husband arrived around 7.30. They said they were going to the local pub for a meal if I'd like to join them. I realized I was hungry – very – and accepted gladly.

The following morning saw me back at the surgery in order to collect not only my screwdriver but also the death certificate, duly signed by two doctors (yes, they *had* managed to find the mortuary), without which I could not obtain a Registration of Death certificate, without which Nigel could not be cremated.

It was, by now, Saturday, a day on which the registrar's office was normally closed, so special arrangements had to be made and the registrar had to open up just for me, which, I imagine, hadn't put him in the best of moods, which manifested itself when I couldn't remember the date on which Nigel and I were married. I was doing quite well in the quiz up to that point, but my mind went a total blank on that one. This apparently was so serious that I had a sudden joyous

hallucination. If I couldn't produce a marriage date, and
Nigel couldn't officially be registered dead without it,
perhaps he wasn't, because legally he couldn't be, and
when I got home I'd find …

I came down to earth again. The registrar was saying
that I must at least remember the year. I didn't, but I
remembered the month: it was September. This piece of
information I gave him with a triumphant smile. My
satisfaction was short-lived. The year of the ceremony
was most definitely required. The registrar was
regarding me over the top of his spectacles and trying not
to look at his watch.

I recalled Nigel's telling me that he got tired of signing
his name, which was a long one, on forms required by
local government each week and for which his office was
responsible, and started signing Karl Marx and Adolf
Hitler and other such notable figures of history. I was
most impressed and asked him if there was ever any
comeback.

'Oh no,' he said. 'All they need to see is a squiggle on
the required line. Nobody ever reads them.'

Smiling broadly again, I said, '1976', which was duly
entered. Later I told Caroline, who said, 'Rubbish! That
was the year *I* was married.' I knew it had *something* to
do with weddings!

The rest of the bank holiday weekend passed slowly. I
remember buying food and drink for the funeral buffet,
and also attending a twenty-fifth wedding anniversary
party on the Saturday evening. The hostess rang and
asked tactfully and hesitantly if I felt like it. I found
myself considering the protocol – an absurdity in the face
of my determination to flout convention with regard to
the funeral arrangements! I accepted and enjoyed it.
Everyone was so sweet and warm and natural with me,
and I felt a deep glow of affection and thankfulness for
my friends. It seemed I had so many.

The long weekend also gave me time to myself to rest
and ponder on all that had gone and was to come. I was
glad that I knew exactly where Nigel was. If he'd gone to

the crematorium mortuary with Alan, there would have
been a blank in my mind, as I had never seen it, and
anyway it was thirty miles away. This was important
somehow. I could get to the car-park in a few minutes if I
wanted to and be near him, thinking of him – his
problems over, lying on the brown eiderdown in his blue
pyjamas. I'd been asked how I wanted him dressed. It
seemed an odd question. 'As he is,' I said. I remembered
that sometimes men are decked out in their best suits
with collars and ties. The thought to me was faintly
obscene. No, it was clothes for the living as far as I was
concerned. I'd take them all to the Salvation Army – if
they'd have them.

I thought I should start packing his clothes straight
away but decided to wait till after the funeral. Instead I
tidied the spare room, glad again that I had been forced,
through circumstances, to have him with me the night
after his death, because to me he wasn't Nigel one
moment because he was breathing and not Nigel the next
because he'd stopped. Not something to be removed as
quickly as possible so that all is decent again and the
proper rituals of mourning can begin.

This sanitization of death is, of course, comparatively
recent. Many people today can remember well when the
bodies of relations were kept in the front room until the
funeral, to be visited by family and friends if they wished,
for a last goodbye. I pondered also on the question as to
why it matters so much to most of us what on earth
(literally) happens to human remains? Christians believe
that the soul goes marching on – they hope to a better
world, and atheists in eternal sleep. So what the Dickens
is it all about? I am aware that these two attitudes are
contradictory, but they exist side by side in my mind and,
I would guess, in the minds of many others. Where death
is concerned, rationality doesn't necessarily fly out of the
window but does appear to hover rather uncertainly over
the sill.

Later I was questioned by a journalist as to how I
would reply to those who spoke of lack of respect in the

way Nigel's body was handled during the twenty-four
hours after his death.

I answered, after some consideration, 'Respect for
what?' Meaning that, if he hadn't managed to earn
respect during his lifetime, no amount afterwards was
going to do him any good.

On Tuesday, the day before the funeral, Alan reminded
me that I should check with the crematorium organist
that he would play the music I had requested, which was
Prokofiev's *Winter Bonfire*. (This had no bearing on the
incinerable nature of the occasion; it was merely a great
favourite of us both.) The organist had said that if there
was an organ, or even a piano transcription of the music,
he would play it. I thought that he could have telephoned
me if it were unobtainable but apparently he hadn't
bothered, and the sheet music was indeed not to be had.

I said, 'In that case, what about *Phantom of the Opera*?'
Yes, he would play that if there was a copy in the
library; if not, would I like his general opera selection? I
wouldn't and said so; to avoid it, I told him I would try to
get the album and bring it to the Wrexham crematorium
that evening. Yellow pages again. Wrexham music shops
did not have it. In Chester one shop had one copy left and
would save it for me if I could get there that afternoon. It
was by now after two, and I had to get the album to the
crematorium by five. This entailed an eighty-mile drive
in all, at a time when I should have been making
sandwiches for the post-funeral bun-fight.

All this effort turned out to be a total waste of time
because, in the event, only a few bars of 'Music of the
Night' wheezed from the instrument, and that so *sotto
voce* that it could scarcely be heard. I should have
specified *forte*.

This is something to be aware of: say you'd like it loud
if you would, otherwise as a mistaken token of respect
you'll hardly hear it. Another point to bear in mind is
that, although many hours of agonizing are often spent
by relations over the choice of music, the actual time

given to tapes or organ-playing in crematoria averages
sixteen seconds. Some will not allow tapes and insist that
if music is required it be played by their contract
organist. Either way, if you blow your nose, you may well
miss it altogether.

Wednesday, the day of the funeral, was dry and bright
but with a chilly breeze. I had arranged my pall-bearers
(all close friends) sometime earlier and instructed them
to meet Alan and Joy in the car-park at 9.45. With the
drinks set out and the food at the ready, I set off with
Caroline, who had arrived from Denmark the night
before. It was the third trip she had made that year,
leaving husband, sons and job to visit her father.

The Volvo was already there when we arrived. The
journey had not been entirely uneventful, I discovered
later. Alan had put a sheet of laminate in the back, so
that the coffin could slide in and out easily and the
bearers would not be involved in an undignified struggle
outside the crematorium doors. Unfortunately, this had
the effect of making it also extremely mobile during
transport, and it was sliding about at every bend in the
road. Joy said that this really wasn't on and that they
must pull up at the side of the road and try to find some
stones or something with which to wedge the coffin. They
stopped and another friend bound for the same place,
who had seen the problem, pulled up and walked over to
them. 'Having trouble with Nigel then?' he said. A quick
consultation and some hefty briefcases were produced,
which answered perfectly.

Alan had asked me to arrive in good time with the
Registration of Death certificate and, equally important
apparently, the cheque, without which the cremation
could not take place. As costs rise, there are several
schemes whereby you can pay now and die later, but not
the reverse. I imagine this is on the grounds that there
can be no profitable reclamation of the goods in default of
settlement!

Owing to my single-handed battle with the sandwiches, I was not late but cutting it a little fine, and Alan

was already in the office writing a cheque when I panted
in. I couldn't resist, 'Are you treating him then?' The cost
was £105, including the organist and £3 for the box for the
ashes, which, I was told, could be collected the next
morning.

Alan had seemed impressed when he made the arrangements that the crematorium officials had been helpful and
raised no objections to the DIY aspect of our undertaking,
though on the whole preferring a coffin to a cardboard
carton or a plastic bag. I couldn't see that this was
especially praiseworthy. After all, they were paid the
same sum whether Nigel arrived by Rolls Royce or
dustcart. It was, however, a month or two before they gave
up sending me colourful brochures with inducements to
have a rose bush planted in his name or an attractively
calligraphed entry in their 'Book of Remembrance', to be
opened every year on the date of his death to com-
memorate his passing etc, etc, none of which was cheap
and I'm sure that neither I nor anyone else who knew him
will need that kind of reminder.

Nigel's will had specified 'garden flowers only'. He'd at
first said, 'wild flowers', but I reminded him of what had
happened at Caroline's wedding. We had held the reception at the melin, and I had conceived the pretty idea of
decorating it throughout with wild flowers. It was July
and the pollen count was high. Need I say more? If so,
imagine the suffering of those poor souls subject to hay
fever, of whom there seemed to be a perversely larger than
average number among our guests. One met them at every
turn asking plaintively, 'Has edyone god edy andihyster-
bine tableds?' A repetition of *that* episode would not, I felt,
have been seemly in the circumstances and would have
reduced me, for one, into a fit of nervous giggles. However,
no money was to be spent on florists' bouquets or wreaths,
and in any case we'd both always hated to see flowers
wired and thrust into stiff, unnatural arrangements. So
all attending had brought their freshly picked bunches
with them and laid them on the coffin as they arrived, and
I must say that it looked – and smelled – lovely.

So the previous party of mourners safely out, our procession started off. I had picked my pall-bearers carefully, so that, for obvious reasons, they would be of more or less uniform height, but one of them was late, and the fourth corner had to be hoisted onto the shoulder of Nigel's nephew, who was six-foot-four-plus-a-bit. At a slightly uneven stagger the coffin set off down the aisle.

Two thoughts were uppermost in my mind. When would the fourth pall-bearer arrive, because, although the labouring side of his assignment was being carried out, he was the first to be called by Alan to say a few words, and also why was the organist playing in such a muted fashion? Music was always played at concert pitch in our house. Nigel was a little deaf, but in any case that was the way he liked it. I was just wondering, having reached my seat, whether I could whip back and tell him to belt it out a bit, when it stopped altogether. The coffin had reached its resting-place and had landed, without disgracing itself, on the catafalque awaiting it. At that moment my fourth pall-bearer and his wife, who had suffered traffic problems, scampered to their seats. And so began what was, to me, a most moving ceremony.

Gavin Miller (late pall-bearer) began his address.

'My dear Jane and friends,' he said, 'I am greatly privileged to have been asked to say a few words today. Indeed, all of us here today are privileged by the fact that we knew Nigel. You and Nigel were the first friends Rita and I made, nine years ago, when we came to live in North Wales. Just as we fell in love at first sight with our new home, so we fell in love with you and Nigel at first meeting. At the time you do not analyse the reasons for love-affairs – they are just instinctive – they just happen.

'Yet today, if I must give reasons for the love-affair we all shared with Nigel, it is not difficult. There was his keen sense of humour; his hospitality; his wide knowledge of so many subjects; his concern for dumb animals; and his contempt for not so dumb humans.

'Recently he showed me a form he had had printed; the

form to stop all forms. It is very funny – a dig at over-pompous officialdom in true Nigel style.

'One thing I had in common with Nigel was our National Health hearing aid. If I have a criticism of the National Health Service, it is that, by mistake, his was tuned into the right while mine was correctly tuned to centre left.*

'So what can we do now that we have lost Nigel? Might I suggest that we ask our MPs to use their influence to stop all advertising and sponsorship of smoking products which are now largely directed at young people?

'And so we express our deep sympathy to Jane and our thanks for the life of Nigel, a life we shall miss very much. "Gentleman" is not a good enough word with which to describe him. Might I say, on your behalf, goodbye to a gentle prince?'

Then it was Alan's turn.

'It was Nigel's wish that his family and friends should, as far as possible in this specialist world, themselves carry out his funeral. That has been faithfully done.

'I met Nigel only a few years ago. During that time he proved to be a wonderful companion. His first-class education, his wide experience of engineering around the world, combined with the speed and clarity of his mind, made conversing with him a delightful privilege. I'm sorry I didn't meet him much earlier.

'He had great hopes for the future development of science and technology and the contribution they will make to the well-being of humanity, on the artistic side, as well as the material world. He revelled in music and had reached a well-matured view of life and people, and was happy.

'The following poem by Tennyson describes perfectly for me both Nigel's life story and his philosophy.

' "Mechenophilus" by Alfred, Lord Tennyson, written in the time of the first railways:

* This is a reference to their opposing political views.

'Now first we stand and understand,
And sunder false from true,
And handle boldly with the hand
And see and shape and do.

Dash back that ocean with a pier,
Strow yonder mountain flat,
A railway there, a tunnel here,
Mix me this zone with that!

Bring me my horse – my horse? my wings
That I may soar the sky,
For thought into the outward springs,
I find her with the eye.

O will she, moonlike, sway the main,
And bring or chase the storm,
Who was a shadow in the brain
And is a living form?

Far as her Future vaults her skies,
From this my vantage ground
To those still-working energies
I spy nor term nor bound.

As we surpass our Father's skill
Our sons will shame our own;
A thousand things are hidden still
And not a hundred known.

And had some prophet spoken true
Of all we shall achieve,
The wonders were so wildly new
That no man would believe.

Meanwhile, my brothers, work and wield
The forces of today,
And plow the Present like a field,
And garner all you may!

You, what the cultured surface grows,
Dispense with careful hands:
Deep under deep for ever goes,
Heaven over heaven expands.

'Jane made Nigel a happy, tranquil man. Our thoughts today and in the future are with her and the rest of his family.

'Much of Nigel's working life was spent making beacons for navigators. His light lives on in our hearts.'

Well, follow that, I thought. I'd been having to dig my nails into the palm of my hand very hard in order to stop the tears streaming, which I couldn't let happen as I was to speak next and needed to keep steady.

I must explain here that, as neither Nigel nor I had religion, I had arranged the two speakers and then planned to say a few words myself, to thank everyone, in and out of sight. I wanted to include his doctors and nurses at both hospitals in which he had been a patient, and our friends in the residential home. I hoped it wouldn't sound too much like an Oscar acceptance speech, but I was determined not to leave anyone out.

That was the plan. But at the eleventh hour I heard that Nigel's stepbrother would be attending, driving up from Somerset and coming straight to the crematorium. He is a retired reverend, and I thought that, as he had made the effort, it might be nice to ask him to say a prayer to round off the proceedings. Also it would be a gesture towards the Christian believers in the congregation, who might otherwise have felt a little cheated.

I sent a message via others of Nigel's relations that, should he do the bit about it 'pleasing Almighty God to take unto himself our dear brother Nigel', he would run the risk of an immediate and very angry protest from me. In the event he said two or three short prayers, which I hope and believe were appreciated.

So I spoke, and the reverend prayed and we all trooped out again. The sun was now high and I noticed how very beautiful were the surroundings. The crematorium had been built in the park of a stately home with cultivated and wild parts, a lake and many mature trees. It covered a large area, and I really wouldn't have minded leaving Nigel there, but the compost heap was what he wanted, and the compost heap was where he was going.

As we filed out, Joy noticed ill-disguised interest on the faces of the undertaker and bearers of the next party waiting for their ceremony (they don't waste time in these places, and you may be penalized if you are late). Their usual professionally lugubrious expressions slipped markedly into stark astonishment, almost disbelief, hoping, no doubt, that this was not a glimpse of the future.

We drove home. Friends came in for a drink and a snack and kept on coming and going for the rest of the day, which was useful as well as friendly because they brought their appetites with them, and most of the refreshments were disposed of.

There was a lot of laughter, not the least when someone asked the whereabouts of Alan and Joy, and I said that Alan had gone to be induced! Words had failed me. What I had meant to say was that he was being inducted as a churchwarden, and the two of them had gone off for the ceremony – my friend was having a busy day! They were soon back, however, to share the joke. It was altogether a very jolly wake.

At last, when they had all gone home, I started woozily and happily to clear up. A great sense of peace descended upon me. It was a perfect summer evening. And we'd done it – *ourselves*. No strangers in black coats, no false pomp and ceremony; just his family, just his friends. I was content.

3   The Broadcast

And so it was all over. A blankness settled over me. Not
happy – not unhappy – just blank. All my thoughts,
actions and energies for the last four months had been
concerned only with Nigel. What Molly Keane, in her
novel *Good Behaviour*, calls 'the anaesthetic of busyness'
had ceased. It was as if an addictive drug had been
withdrawn and I was faced with the reality of life and
had forgotten what to do with it. There were, of course,
the inevitable forms to fill in and letters of condolence to
answer, but I realized that I had not for a moment, since
before the previous Christmas, given a thought to the
prospect of life for one.

Joy and Alan set off on one of their marathon walks,
this time a coast-to-coast sponsored effort to raise money
for our local church, one of the oldest in North Wales. I
had known that this was pending but when, over the last
few weeks, I had enquired when they were going to start
out, the reply was always the same, 'Oh, I think we'll
wait a bit and hope for some warmer weather.' Actually I
had come to realize that they were, in fact, 'waiting' for
Nigel. I hoped that the walk was the pleasant relaxation
they always claimed that these expeditions were. How
they deserved, and must have needed, it.

Among the many 'thank-you' letters I wrote, I sent one
to Alan Shell of the Humanist Association, who replied,
'We are very glad our letter was of help to you and you
will be interested to know that I propose to send copies of

your letter, with your name deleted, to our funeral officiants in the hope that they will take courage from it and help any others who might be in similar difficulties.'

I wasn't too sure what 'officiants' were in this context but have since realized that they perform in place of ministers of religion in humanist funerals.

I had duly collected Nigel's ashes. This was a shock. For some reason I'd thought I'd be given just a sample in a small box – like those used to send out wedding cake. The parcel with which I was presented was the size of a largeish shoe-box and surprisingly heavy. Of course, I thought, it's the ashes of the coffin as well, so it would be quite a weight. I put the brown paper parcel on the chest in the hall, waiting, I told myself, for a less rainy/windy/busy day, but really because I was funking it.

I knew I must soon arrange the memorial party, and the perfect opportunity arose with a letter from one of my closest friends, Margo, now living in Australia, who was planning a trip to Europe with her husband later that summer. They would be with me for four days in July.

I had known Margo since she was fifteen. She was a talented ice-skater who was then playing her first principal role in the Wembley pantomime *Dick Whittington On Ice*. I dubbed her voice. For those who do not know, the voices of skaters in these huge arenas are always dubbed. Recording had proved to be useless, because if a skater fell or was late on an entrance the sound of his or her voice carrying on the dialogue with unaware insouciance was pretty bizarre. It was a new source of work for actors and singers for which there was much gratitude. I did many such shows.

Margo went from strength to strength, with bigger and better parts, but after a few years turned to acting and much later married an Australian singer/actor, Rod McLennon, and went to live in Melbourne. She was an attractive, kind, intelligent and above all practical person whom I was particularly glad to have around at such a time. Margo and Nigel had always been very fond of each other, and she was upset to have missed him.

I got cracking. I realized I'd no experience of organizing a memorial party and didn't know anybody who had. I began to make a list. I started with the drinks. That was easy – lots of everything. 'A jolly good booze-up,' Nigel had said. Well, we'd have it. What about a cake? Did one in such circumstances? Well, it was a celebration of his life, wasn't it? I decided to order one – a fruit cake – from a local café, the Sospan Fach (Little Saucepan). I explained what I wanted and arranged a date on which I would collect it. When I did so, I was told there was no charge. Now this was a lady who hardly knew me and had met Nigel only once, and briefly, at a party. The now-familiar lump in my throat welled up again.

A nurse who had cared devotedly for Nigel when he was at home agreed to ice it for me. It was simple and, to my mind, quite beautiful. White with deep red roses, his initials, N.L.S., on the top and the dates of his birth and death round the side in silver.

The party, which was confined to local friends owing to the remoteness of our village from the metropolis, was, I think, very successful and just the kind of gathering Nigel loved. The following morning, under the guidance of Margo, Nigel was sprinkled onto the compost heap and we said our final goodbyes. The engineer with the irreverent sense of humour who wouldn't give house-room to a defunct machine but who would carefully dismantle and put by any parts that might be of use later on would – this time next year – be helping to nourish the rose beds.

In September BBC Radio 4 announced the planning of a new programme. Consumer-orientated, it invited listeners to write in about anything they had found difficult to buy or do and were wanting to know why. The BBC would then give them help to find out. 'It's your programme, just the way you want it,' and 'the programme in which *you* set the agenda,' said the announcer. The third time I heard this trail (as they are called), I dashed off a quick letter about my coffin difficulties, asking, at the same time, that if the producer considered my problem worth airing, could I be provided with a tape-recorder so I could get some of the more pompous prevarications dished out by the trade on permanent record? I then went off on holiday and forgot all about it.

My destination was Welcombe in North Devon, a place introduced to me by Nigel, who had lived there during the early part of the war. During his time there, ostensibly farming, Nigel restored, almost single-handedly and certainly single-mindedly, a decayed waterwheel at Docton Mill, not far from Welcombe in the parish of Hartland, which belonged to his friend Ronnie Duncan's mother and sister. Long after he left to become a flight engineer it continued to light them through the war and for many years after. Following their deaths, Ronnie sold Docton to a man who was keen to get the wheel going again and, with Nigel's assistance and local labour, the second restoration was started and we both made new friends in Steve and Iris Pugh. Nigel was, by this time, unable to do much in the way of hulking and heaving, owing to having suffered from the fashionable slipped disc eighteen years earlier, which still had to be watched. Nevertheless, he designed and wired the control panel and delighted both in his consultant capacity and also in being again involved in his life's obsession on what to him was virtually home ground.

Nigel has left more than one thumbprint of his time in North Devon. The other is a motor of highly original design (for the conversant, one without commutator or armature), one of which now carries the great lens on Lundy North lighthouse that warns sailors of the savage coastline of the area.

I had been visiting Welcombe with Nigel since 1960. I knew it wasn't going to be easy, as it was so very much his world, but I realized I must do it soon, because the longer I delayed, the longer I felt I would go on doing so – like facing up to the ashes. I was glad I did. All his old friends seemed pleased to see me, and the place lived up to its name. It wasn't really as hard as I thought it would be. Again, just like the ashes.

When I got home I found, among the mountain of letters (mainly telling me I had filled in a blue form when it should have been a yellow one or asking for information I had already given), one from the BBC asking me to get in touch with the *Punters* office in Bristol as soon as possible. I telephoned the next day, and the producer, having chatted with me awhile and ascertained that I was not a nutter (I think), asked me to make a programme. I was to have not only a tape-recorder but a minder as well to guide me through the intricacies and, I imagine, the possible legal hazards of broadcasting such an item; he and his lady assistant would arrive and spend a day with me the following week. I would also be required to go to Bristol a couple of days later to do some work in the studio and, I assumed, to help with the editing. It sounded interesting.

The day came – it was 19 October 1987 – and my minder/presenter and his young lady assistant arrived. He explained the format. He also explained that I must talk freely and not be intimidated by the recording machine. 'Tape is very cheap,' he said kindly. Was this the point at which to say that I had been a professional actress for over thirty years and was well aware of the mechanics etc? I thought not. It had little relevance. After all, in my job I had learned and spoken another people's words, and here I was, reduced to my own. Luckily I turned out to be reasonably fluent and uninhibited when expressing my own thoughts and feelings.

I told my story with the help of Joy and Alan, who arrived for coffee and contributed greatly with their humanity, humour and charm. Joy retold how the problem of how the mobile coffin in transit was resolved, and Alan spoke movingly about his feelings for Nigel and about the whole concept of a DIY funeral. He said, 'I'd talked so much to Nigel about his thoughts on so many things that as far as I'm concerned he was with us all the

way through. It was a question of faith – keeping faith all
the way. There were times when it was a strain, but you
had in the front of your mind that this was for your
friend, and that deepened the friendship.'

After a pub lunch we did a bit outside the car-park
mortuary and then settled down with the telephone to
record some attempts to buy a coffin, one of which
resulted in agreement, which was the last thing we
needed at the time, although it came in very handy later.
The rest of the traders, however, again expressed
shock/horror at the very idea and were usefully
sententious with it. Then we set off by car to tape some
face-to-face interviews with funeral directors. These
performed just as required, with pious platitudes
followed by prevaricating and tut-tutting in a most
gratifying manner. The BBC and I finally bade each
other goodnight at 6.30, with what seemed to be a good
day's work on the cassettes.

Perhaps I should take up this investigative journalism.
Eat your heart out, Roger Cook! I often have this type of
fantasy when very tired, and that certainly I was. In the
morning I remembered that Roger Cook sometimes gets
thumped – quite hard, and abandoned the idea.

The day in Bristol was also busy. I drove down the
afternoon before and was put up in a small hotel near the
studios. Called to attend at 10.15 in the morning, we
started in the time-honoured way of civilization with a
coffee break. Then more telephone calls.

First an interview with Richard Buckley, a retired
funeral director, who had written the paragraph in *It's a
R.I.P. Off* which first aroused our interest in the subject.
He explained that, since he wrote that advice, it was
getting more difficult to arrange a DIY funeral because of
the growing number of takeovers; in fact, three
companies between them had large parts of the southern
half of the country sewn up. They now not only conduct
funerals but have their own joiners and monumental
masons making coffins and headstones, and some even
own their own crematoria. It is easy to see that would-be

DIY funeral undertakers would be as welcome as a swarm of greenfly at the Chelsea flower show.

Next to Howard Hodgson, known at the time as the tycoon of funeral directors. Hodgson Holdings was then the biggest quoted funeral director in Britain, handling one in every twenty funerals nationwide, although the Co-op is still the biggest throughout the British Isles, doing about twenty-five per cent of all funerals. It seems there is an impression that the Co-op is, if not exactly a charity, is certainly some kind of philanthropic organization, so it must follow that their funerals are cheaper. This is not the case. Nevertheless I have since been informed by Richard Buckley that (if the concept is not entirely meaningless in the circumstances) the Co-op gives 'the best value for money', in terms of materials used in their coffins and the general finish and quality of the handles and name-plate etc.

Mr Hodgson explained that in buying up so many small firms, who really could no longer make ends meet, he, Howard Hodgson, could do better and cheaper funerals and that no one need worry about the cost any way, because if the deceased or whoever was taking the responsibility of next-of-kin possessed less than £300, the DHSS would pay for the whole thing. (This figure has now been increased to £500.)

When he finally paused for breath, I said, 'Hold on a moment' and explained that, although obviously nobody wants to spend more than they have to on anything, in my case it was a matter of principle, because I wanted my husband's funeral to be a personal affair in which he would be ministered to by his loved-ones, not strangers. His reply was rather off the point, I thought. It was that if I wanted to set up in the business of manufacturing coffins, he would have no objections. I felt that this conversation was adding little to my, or my listeners', knowledge of how to buy a coffin, so I thanked him kindly for his time and said goodbye.

In the event, none of the interview was included in the broadcast. Perhaps the producer thought the gentleman

had had enough media exposure for a while, as I was given
to understand that he had been granted quite a bit of air
time one way and another in the recent past.

Back in the BBC studios there came next some interesting telephone interviews with the press and public
relations offices of DIY superstores on the subject of their
considering adding coffins to their other self-assembly
furniture. Two refused to talk, having been told they were
being recorded (which is mandatory procedure at the Beeb
and quite rightly). Sainsbury's asked for our number and
said they would call us back. Full marks for training there
– after all, anyone could say they were calling under the
auspices of the BBC. A fourth, after asking if it were April
the first, collapsed into giggles and hung up. I had a quite
reasonable chat with a manager of Texas Home Care, who
said the suggestion was 'a little offbeat' but agreed to put it
to his bosses for consideration. (Since then I have been in
touch with Texas four times and been promised an answer
for which I am still waiting after nearly four years).
Perhaps if, as I am told, they are a branch of Ladbrokes,
they are hedging their bets, i.e. waiting to see if any other
company takes the first step!

In my letter applying to the BBC I had said that I would
also like to telephone several undertakers for quotes,
stating my exact requirements and then taking the
lowest, getting back to them and seeing if they could be
beaten down. This was now attempted, but I got nowhere
near finding out, because none of them would estimate
over the phone. Obviously this kind of shopping around
would not be tolerated: 'your place or mine' was the drill in
every case, with, I inferred, a preference for yours. The
reason for this, I later discovered, is that at yours there is
likely to be a selection of friends and relations, one of
whom in the course of discussion is bound to say, 'Come on,
let's give him the best!' and although he or she is very
seldom the one who is paying for it, no one likes to appear
mean at such a time – an attitude, I might add, of which
the undertaker thoroughly approves!

After a further telephone interview – this time with

myself as the interviewee – for the *Radio Times*, it seemed I was finished. No mention was made of my helping with the editing, and when I enquired, I was told the programme was nowhere near that stage yet; in fact, the producer had not yet had time to listen to the – what must be by now – at least four hours of tape. So I collected my expenses and went home.

The programme was scheduled for mid-November. I wondered what the reaction would be, if any. There was a distinct possibility that it could sink without trace, weighed down by listeners' indifference, or, of course, it might possibly cause a public outcry, disgusting not merely Tunbridge Wells.

On 12 November the programme went on the air. There were parts I would not have selected and others left out that I would have included, but as the whole thing had to be condensed into twenty minutes, I was reasonably pleased with it. The reaction of friends and relations was generally quite favourable and, as it came my way, an interesting and unexpected fact started to emerge. It was the committed Christians who were, in the main, sympathetic, and the dedicated atheists who thought it 'in rather poor taste'. This was not invariable, but common enough to be worthy of note. I hope one day some research may be done on the subject.

One point about the recording worried me. There was no mention of Nigel's final destination, i.e. the compost heap. After all, it was, if not the crux of the whole enterprise, an extremely important component, because his purpose in this was no eccentric whim but a sincere manifestation of the philosophy which had pervaded most of his adult life and which was clear to all who knew him – namely, the conservation of our precious resources. Did the producer, perhaps feel it to be in poor taste? She should maybe have heeded the lyrics of 'On Ilkley Moor Baht 'at', which I discovered, only a very short while ago, I admit, is all about recycling.

It goes:

Verse 1 Where has tha' bin since I saw thee?
On Ilkley Moor baht 'at.
Where has tha' been since I saw thee?
Where has tha' been since I saw thee?
On Ilkley Moor baht 'at,
On Ilkley Moor baht 'at.
Verse 2 Tha's bin a courtin' Mary Jane *etc*.
Verse 3 Tha'll go and catch that death o'cold *etc*.
Verse 4 Then we shall have to bury thee *etc*.
Verse 5 Then worms'll come and eat thee up *etc*.
Verse 6 Then ducks'll come and eat up worms *etc*.
Verse 7 Then we shall come and eat up ducks *etc*.
Verse 8 Then we shall all have eaten thee. *etc*.

Also Cruse, 'The National Organization for the Widowed and their Children', publishes an anthology for the bereaved called 'All in the end is Harvest'. Looked at in this light, and with conservation so constantly impressed upon us, I really can't see that the idea could be so shocking. Perhaps I should be charitable and put the omission down to some other reason.

One surprise offer came my way as a direct result. I had decided that, much to my regret, it would not be possible to plan a DIY funeral for myself as it was not a job I would bequeath to friends, and my nearest close relations who might have co-operated were overseas. However, out of the blue came the offer of a friend to do it for me, and naturally I accepted gratefully. I remembered the name of the manufacturer who'd said 'yes' on the telephone, and two days later drove off in the Metro and picked out my coffin. To my surprise, by dint of my putting down the front seat, it fitted inside the car, so the public was spared the probably unusual sight of a coffin on a roof-rack. Once it was home, the stalwart Alan helped me up to the loft with it, where it awaits my occupation in due course. I wondered, when I set off to get it, if my notoriety had been communicated on the jungle drums and if the promised purchase might still elude me, so I was especially glad to have it safely at home.

I was asked once if it seemed real to me that one day I
would be lifeless inside it. In other words, could I truly
visualize my own death? I tried to think about this but
didn't succeed. It seemed remote to the point of
impossibility. Also, what was there to think? It wasn't
like visualizing a holiday – even a place one hasn't been
before; after all, there are certain immutables: land, sea,
sky and clouds (not too many of these, please); and even
should one have chosen a more unusual location, such as
the Arctic or the Gobi Desert, there are photographs.
Man knew more about the landscape of the moon before
the first landing than we know about 'afterlife'. I would
defy even Elizabeth Kubler-Ross, an American 'death
expert', who was shown on TV recently, to know much
about it. All we have are conflicting beliefs – no solid
facts, so thinking about one's death seems an impossibility. When one tries, one finds oneself a spectator at the
event. The deathbed scene; the funeral; the sadness of
friends, and the smugness of certain relations who never
liked you much and have outlived you (just wait till my
will is read!). Dying is, of course, different. For myself, I
hope to accomplish it without too much pain, and with
present-day drug developments this seems probable. But
death ...? One can only speculate, and surely there's a
more constructive way to spend one's time?

A week passed. So that was that. It caused a bit of a buzz
locally but, I thought, would soon be deposed as a
talking-point by the next raffle to be drawn in aid of
renovating the Pavilion or the latest radiation figures on
Chernobyled sheep.
   Yes, that really is what I thought.

4   The Response

'The broadcast was amazing – astounding! The impact seems to have been far and wide.'

'I sat absolutely riveted.'

'Such courage and good sense.'

'Enormous admiration for showing us what a ride we are taken for by the funeral directors. After all, we don't pay to be born – why so much to die?'

'I hope something will be done now your programme has highlighted the fact that we don't have to conform.'

'An amazing story told with great skill and restraint.'

'Very funny and incredibly moving. Her courage, determination, wit and gift for life were beyond praise.'

Gosh! Well! I mean ... well ... Gosh!

The above quotations are part of a large batch of letters forwarded from the BBC which arrived on my mat ten days after the programme went out. They were enclosed with a letter from the producer of the series, who wrote: 'As we answered the phones to a delighted public I realized that you have said what masses of people always wanted to hear.'

I was very pleased, naturally, but the task of answering them all, which I was determined to do, was daunting, to say the least. I decided to do half a dozen a day until I'd got through them. The trouble was they kept on coming. Many were quickly dealt with, just a 'Thank you so much', but others seemed to regard me as some sort of authority and requested: 'Further details, please.

SAE enclosed.' I did my best. Certain information asked for, I simply did not have. I could see there was more work looming. In the midst of life I was unquestionably in the midst of death.

There were requests for interviews from journalists. Two correspondents wanted to write plays – one for TV and the other radio. A third fancied a documentary reconstruction, and the more the publicity, the more the letters came thumping onto the mat. A centre spread in the *Evening Standard* brought a new cascade. People were realizing that they had a choice.

Central Television came and made an interview/ documentary film for their weekly current affairs programme *Central Lobby*, during the course of which I was seen driving around the neighbourhood, first preceding and then followed by the camera crew. It was useless to protest that the coffin fitted comfortably into the car with the back door closed. 'We can't see it like that, Jane,' I was told. So the not-every-day sight of a coffin sticking up out of the hatch-back of a Metro was duly recorded. Next morning the compost heap was photographed, and off they went back to Birmingham.

When it was shown, I booked into an hotel in Shrewsbury, not being able to receive it in my area, and watched it in the seclusion of a pleasant bedroom. It was well done, I thought, without sensationalism or sentimentality. I had become a current affair – how odd!

I was interviewed by *Living* magazine (no, the irony did not escape me) and also by *The Independent*, which published the feature in a section under the same name!

It is just not realized that it is possible or even legal to arrange a funeral without employing undertakers – a gap in public knowledge which, of course, the undertakers do little to fill. The phrase 'It never occurred to me' was repeated in letter after letter. The many other points made, and reasons given, are best, I think, left to my correspondents themselves to express; here is a further sample of the most recurrent.

From a gentleman in Hornchurch:

In our own recent experiences of three family funerals, the actions of the Ministers, and attitudes of funeral directors only added further grief and distress to the proceedings. Next of kin and mourners are treated like morons who really shouldn't be there, as they only delay things and interfere with *their* role, and any change suggested, or interest expressed in the proceedings by the mourners, is totally unacceptable. It was like a factory line to which we all had to conform. Given scant information, one is expected to accept their procedures without question, and then pay inflated bills because everyone else does. I so wish that our love and respect for the deceased could have been expressed openly, and with joy and gratitude the way yours was. Your suggestion of flat pack, self assembly coffins on sale in supermarkets is marvellous. I do hope the idea catches on, with other requirements purchased separately, as needed, as you did.

And from a lady in Putney: 'Why kill trees for coffins? Surely heavy plastic bags would do just as well?'

Another in Sutton, Surrey, said: 'I would only want a bunch of wild flowers and the simplest departure possible. I'm sure your husband appreciated from afar the care and "antics" of you and your friends, the personal and loving touch that one would give to any loved one going on a long journey.'

Then a mother from Clwyd in Wales: 'I am fully in agreement with her motives. When our second child was very ill, the most distressing thought was that total strangers would be the last to touch him. Has she thought of setting up in the coffin business herself? Someone should.'

And a lady writing from Bristol, who achieved a DIY funeral herself: 'Keeping the funeral in the family made it warm and home-like. The home-made aspect makes the relinquishing of the dead much easier and much more a part of life. My man had an abhorrence of show and pomp and hypocrisy, and would have so enjoyed the moments

of absurdity and humour. Also, it was good to be busy at
such a time. It must be awful to have it all taken out of
one's hands and have nothing to do but wait – and for
what? A macabre and hypocritical circus.'

A clergyman's wife in Sheffield said: 'A DIY funeral –
why not? For far too long the undertakers have had the
monopoly. They seem to prey (forgive the pun) on the
bereaved at a time of distress. If it catches on it will
certainly be one in the eye for greedy undertakers – after
all, you never see a poor one, do you?'

Also from a like-minded member of a large family, all
of whom intend DIY funerals: 'I am one of eight children.
My parents are alive and have thirty grandchildren. We
all intend to have DIY funerals and our coffins made by a
carpenter. My father will be buried at sea. I hope you get
a positive response from listeners. We all have to die.
Why is everyone so coy?'

A wife in Shrewsbury said: 'My husband and I are both
cynical about the monopoly of funeral directors and their
sincerity. For instance one even billed for a glass of
sherry partaken in his office! It seems that the essential
ingredient in all this is a Volvo. A purpose for which I
guess even Volvo have not taken into account in their
advertising budget!' (In this last sentence the lady is not
quite accurate. A large percentage of hearses are indeed
diesel Volvos sprayed black.)

And this correspondent, to whom, sadly, I could not
reply because she didn't give her full address: 'Fantastic,
exactly the way I would like my funeral arranged. Over
the counter coffins? Yes, definitely. How wonderful to
think only friends and family need be involved.'

And this gentleman in West Yorkshire would certainly
have the blessing of many if he carried out his idea:
'Having taken early retirement, I am casting about for
some way to supplement my pension. It occurs to me that
"mail order coffin supply" might be a suitable avenue to
explore.'

And one from Scotland represents the philanthropists'
view: 'We would prefer to depart in plain, "off the rack",

coffins and so allow the savings to be devoted to charity. This is the age of change. Come on somebody, be enterprising!'

And this one from a most complimentary lady in Northampton: 'I hope the programme will give lots of people the determination to persevere as you did. I'm sure your husband is proud of you. With much admiration and I hope you are inundated with letters.' Yes, well, the hope of *that* writer was fully realized!

Some of the most gratifying comments referred to Nigel – such as, 'How you achieved that much wished objective said as much about your late husband as it did about you. He must have been a quite remarkable man.'

Another greatly pleasurable result of the broadcast was that it put me in touch with colleagues of his, and their wives, in the lighthouse business, several of whom wrote me the kindest letters expressing the most heart-warming comments. To quote again: 'Nigel would have been so proud of you.' And: 'Nigel would have been delighted at your success and I was very moved by your point that at no time was he attended or touched by any but those close to him. I venture to add that this must be the greatest labour of love that anyone can render to a friend. I wish I had been able to help. Also you struck a whacking blow on his behalf against the sort of people he particularly disliked.'

'I have a feeling you have begun something that will keep you busy for quite some time to come.' No kidding! I had that feeling too.

There were letters offering practical help. Among them a man who turned out to be an embalmer and whose advice and information were most useful. He told me some hair-raising stories of the casual, careless way in which bodies can be handled at the undertaker's and in transit, the most common being losing the coffin on the way to the funeral because the doors have not been properly secured or the wrong name-plates having been attached, resulting in great distress to the relations of the deceased and confusion for the minister concerned, all of which made our dealings with Nigel seem positively reverential!

Nor are undertakers alone in careless and callous behaviour. Hospitals must also take their share of criticism. A correspondent told me of her visit to a hospital mortuary to identify her 20-year-old daughter, who had been killed in a car crash. This she was required to do from behind a glass screen and, having done so, was immediately ushered out. It did not occur to her until later that she could have asked to touch her daughter or kiss her goodbye, as her instinct urged. She was, of course, within her rights to do this, but the fact that this courtesy is not offered is customary and, in my opinion, unfeeling in the extreme. In this situation the next-of-kin really is in a state of total shock and incapable of cogent thought and should therefore be given every opportunity to express whatever grief is felt that will help to assuage their loss.

However, the reverse of this experience was reported to me by a woman who lost her lover in a drowning accident. She told how she was encouraged to go to the hospital mortuary each day and sit with him until, as she said, 'I felt ready to let him go.' But this was in Australia.

In a recent study, *Matters of Life and Death*, South Birmingham Community Health Council carried out a survey of bereavement experiences. Several examples of lack of sensitivity and support were reported in the *Guardian*. One parent was told by a consultant, 'We all have to go sometime,' after her 16-year-old son had just died of leukaemia. Another was told to 'snap out of it'. Yet another to 'hurry up', when taken to see her husband's body. Another statement quoted – and this, to me, is in a way the most shocking – was: 'It was obviously just part of their job ... No one seemed to appreciate that the "body" they were discussing was actually the person I loved.'

My vet, Jackie, has a great deal more empathy. When she finally had to put down my old cat Mrs, she said afterwards, 'Would you like to stay and be alone with her for a while? I've no one coming for half an hour.'

The dying themselves will nearly always let it be

known, albeit tacitly, whether or not they want the truth. The signs are not at all difficult to pick up. Jackie told me, regarding my old and much-loved sheepdog Ffly, 'Don't worry, she's in no pain, and she'll let you know when the day comes.' She was right. The intimations were unmistakable, and I telephoned Jackie to come and administer the last rites (so to speak).

There is, at the present time, a movement to tell the patient when they have a terminal illness. 'The dying have a right to know' is the attitude. Admittedly over ninety per cent of people who took part in a survey said that they would want to be told; but it is important to stress that the respondents were all *healthy* people, and in illness attitudes may change. The need to survive is, after all, the most basic instinct we have, and it is necessary to use one's powers of intuition to detect the change of mind which may well accompany the facing of possible extinction. Modern drugs, developed to mitigate some of the more distressing symptoms, can often effect a change of attitude to the extremely hopeful and positive, as was the case with Nigel.

The nice embalmer who wrote to me told me, greatly to his credit, of the totally unnecessary embalming that is frequently carried out, so that the first the next-of-kin knows about it is when he or she receives the bill. If the bill is itemized (which is most unlikely), embalming will probably be entered as 'preservative' or 'hygienic treatment', and if it is discussed with relations when arranging a funeral, an undertaker will often push it as necessary to health. This is total rubbish, as if the body is to be buried or cremated within a few days after death, no such risk exists.

Embalming is a method of temporary preservation, by which process the blood is replaced by a solution of chemicals. In a mortuary, bodies are preserved by refrigeration, which is equally effective and, to be fair, some undertakers use this method. But for an undertaker to insist that both, or even either, are

necessary for public health, except in a tiny minority of
instances, is not true. The only occasion when you won't
get far without it is when the deceased is being sent
abroad. Here again, it is not a legal requirement, but
most airlines insist on it, and a certificate stating that
this has been done must accompany the coffin. The
transport of such cargo is an expensive undertaking, and
some airlines charge twice their usual rate for the
service.

It is true that embalming improves the appearance of a
corpse if it is to be viewed by friends and relations. The
normal hollowing and shrinking of the flesh are arrested,
and it appears firm and lifelike again. The skin colouring
is restored by the use of cosmetics, and the hair
shampooed and set. But once this glitzy transformation
scene is set and the curtain goes up, there is a problem.
Few, in Britain, want the 'open casket' so beloved of the
North Americans and many Continentals. Where is the
audience for this sleeping beauty?

Whatever our conscious reasons ('No, I want to
remember him/her the way he/she was' or 'Not in front of
the children'), a dead body is not considered to be
spectacle for display in Britain, and the rationale which
dictates it can sometimes disguise feelings of embarrassment that such a thing could occur in our death-defying,
well-regulated households. If the death takes place in
hospital, the same will apply. The undertaker will, as a
rule, be instructed to take the body straight to his
premises and screw the lid down, firmly and finally. This
attitude is often, albeit unconscious, a fear of infection.
Not infection in a literal sense of catching whatever
killed Mother – after all, she may have died perfectly
peacefully from old age – but the fear of infection of death
itself, an unpleasant reminder of our own mortality. So
out of sight and out of mind go the innocent wooden box
and its equally innocent contents.

Therefore, if there is no risk to health and no one to see
the deceased, what is this embalming – sorry, 'hygienic
treatment' – business all about? After all, embalming is

strictly forbidden by the Jewish religion, and the Jewish laws on hygiene are among the most stringent in the world. Well, it's about making money.

When Jessica Mitford wrote her informative and wonderfully funny *The American Way of Death*, embalming was not common in Britain. It was not, she said, easy even to obtain embalming materials. There was a distinct risk that an import licence might be refused, for one thing; also the medical profession was, and is, against it, if only because it could prolong the, to them, archaic practice of burying the dead. To doctors, cremation is the only 'hygienic treatment' of corpses which they fully approve.

Since the publication of Miss Mitford's book, unbelievably, more than twenty-eight years ago, some things have greatly changed. In a recent catalogue of a large funeral directors' suppliers firm I counted 309 embalming preparations. These were in sections headed 'Embalming fluids and chemicals', 'Embalming instruments', 'Embalming sundries' and finally 'Cosmetics', which included Velvatone skin lotion, Soft Touch liquid powder, lip wax and Surface restorer in twelve 'complexion co-ordinated shades'. All we lack now is the mechanism to turn these highly decorative cadavers into walkie, if not talkie, zombies, to enable them to give a truly remarkable mannequin parade and show off their mortuary gowns in white polyester and cotton, trimmed with lace and ruffles for ladies and satin quilting for the gents! How *we* managed without all these aids – in fact by merely buying a coffin and getting on with it – I can't imagine, but I know that we were lucky to be living in the UK and not the US, where the open coffin, or at least one quarter open at the head end, is *de rigueur*.

But the embalmers are gaining ground fast, probably because the public does not realize it is happening. A contributor to the *Funeral Service Journal* who declares himself to be 'a devoted and qualified embalmer and tutor' is a funeral director who has recently been giving advice to readers. He suggests that the word 'embalming' should, whenever possible, be avoided and that 'sanitary preparation' and 'hygienic treatment' are little better by way of description. He recommends the phrase 'care of the body' to be used in discussion with clients and continues to surprise us by telling us that in his experience of funeral-arranging he has never yet had anything but a positive response to, 'Would you like us to look after mother in our usual way, so that you will be assured of having an everlasting memory of her sleeping peacefully and at rest?' It would take a very determined and practical mind to say 'No' or even 'How much?'

The sooner the embalming can take place, the easier it is to carry out. Those advocating embalming lose little love for doctors who ask relations for permission to do a post-mortem examination and get it. This cadaver will call for more extensive 'treatment' by the embalmer, due partly to the delay it causes and partly because what is perceived by him to be often unwarranted mutilation. In fact the writer goes on to say, 'It would be the embalmer's dream never to see another "posted case", and he would like to see the usual procedure altered with regard to the requesting of a post-mortem examination. He maintains that, 'So soon after the death of a relative in hospital the next of kin are in the early stages of severe grieving, and often do not understand what is being asked of them.' Referring back to his own audacious euphemisms with regard to 'looking after mother', this is a bit rich.

The following month, in the same journal, a swift refutation of these tenets came in the shape of a letter from a consultant histopathologist by name of J.V. Clark, who responds to the last point regarding the relations' not understanding what is being asked when a post-mortem is requested, by pointing out that in all probability funeral directors do not explain the procedure of embalming to the next of kin and, more seriously, maintaining that delay would reduce the maximum benefit of an autopsy and also delay the funeral.

Hospital post-mortems, he goes on, are requested as a method of monitoring diagnostic technique and refining clinical skills. It is living patients who benefit, and therefore granting permission for a hospital autopsy on one's deceased loved-one is a responsible and public-spirited act, which may benefit other patients. He adds that, unlike the autopsy, 'I can see no benefit in embalming to anyone but the embalmer. Provided there is no prolonged interval between death and the funeral, and provided bodies are kept refrigerated, then embalming, as a hygienic measure, is totally unnecessary. It would be better if all funeral directors provided refrigerated body storage rather than resorted to embalming.' This correspondence, it appears, could continue for some time.

In the USA, I discovered from a report by Dermot Pungavie in the *Daily Mail*, for those mourners who wish to view but are short of time, one funeral director in Chicago has come up with the novel idea of drive-in viewing. It works like this. A carload of friends and relations drive up to his premises, sign a visitors' book and ring for service. A technician using the speakerphone will ask which of his residents you wish to view. The head of the deceased then appears on a television screen which is tastefully draped in white silk and discreetly illuminated at night. This picture remains on the screen for an initial three seconds. If longer is required, further to admire the art work carried out by the local mortician/beautician, you merely press a button and are then given another three seconds. There is no limit to the number of times the button may be pressed, and it seems that mourners in cars queueing behind can get somewhat restive.

Another snag, which it appears was not anticipated, concerns viewing by busload. One deceased of advanced years was visited by many elderly friends, some of whom were not too mobile, and a specially adapted bus was engaged to accommodate their wheelchairs. Having driven past in the usual manner, the driver then had to go through a second time in reverse so that the mourners on the other side could also take a look. However, I'm

sure that it will be only a short time before the
imaginative gentleman of this funeral business (or
after-care service, as it apparently now likes to be called)
will overcome these problems that in any case may be
outweighed by one great advantage to which he points
with pride: namely, that it is above all discreet, in that
the girlfriend of the departed may view at any time,
giving any name, and the wife and family will be none
the wiser!

The BBC telephoned. Could I let them have the exact
name of the coffin-manufacturers who had supplied me,
as they had been inundated with calls asking for it and,
having no success with the number supplied by Directory
Enquiries, were needing further information. Odd, I
thought, as I confirmed the number which they had been
given. I suggested they try again and this time ask for
the man who had signed my receipt, and please – come
back to me and tell me what they say.

Perhaps it will come as no surprise to my readers to
hear not only that all knowledge of selling me a coffin
was denied but even that they were now, or ever had
been, coffin-manufacturers. The funeral directors' lobby
is very strong; I suppose it was naïve of me not to have
realized before that they would clamp down hard on any
wholesaler who dared to step out of line and supply the
public direct. Perhaps they would feel differently if,
instead of an average order of ten or twenty coffins, one of
the superstores came up with one for a thousand.

With so much interest in my activities, it seemed only
fair to try to help others to have a go also. To that end, I
felt, it must be back to the DIY stores. Somehow they
must be made to realize that it would be meeting a
demand, a creditably innovative idea and not immoral,
illegal or fattening, which really would make life, and
death, a lot easier and cheaper for many.

I had, by this time, had a design for a coffin in reasonably priced veneered chipboard sent to me by an interested listener. It is a straight-sided 'casket' type, the

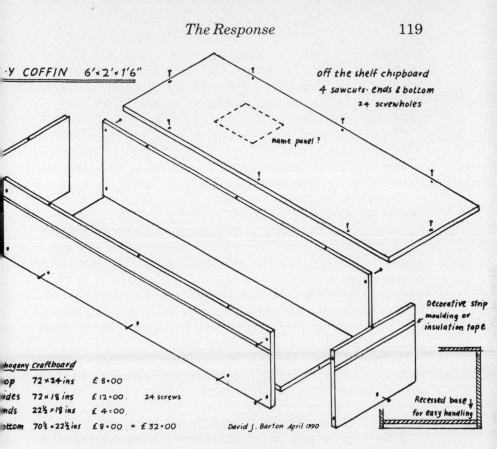

A DIY coffin designed by David J. Barton.

kind preferred on the Continent. This would be easier to
flat-pack and cost the maker exactly £22, constructing it
entirely by hand and purchasing all materials at retail
prices from his local DIY store, thereby, I hoped, proving
that a very comfortable profit could be made while still
considerably undercutting the funeral directors. This
model would, of course, be the cheapest possible for
cremation; anything more elaborate would require to be
of a different design and materials.

Here it might be worth pointing out that handles are
necessary only for burial, for lowering the coffin on ropes
into the grave; for cremation they are quite superfluous.

Also the lining, the types and varieties of which are many, is quite unnecessary! The coffin itself should have the joints sealed with paraffin or similar wax on the inside, and no more is needed. Everything else is just an embellishment.

The coffin design I had photocopied and planned to enclose, along with quotes from correspondents, to several of the DIY superstores.

Incidentally, I telephoned Harrods to enquire what their cheapest chipboard coffin would be, to which the answer was £190!

I spent an interesting afternoon on the telephone trying to elicit the names and addresses of the managing directors of the half-dozen or so biggest DIY chains. One switchboard operator said that at this moment in time she didn't know. I pointed out that it would be difficult to find a moment out of time, even if I could wait for it, and could she find someone who *would* know? On only one occasion was I given an address, and had to be content with those of head offices. Quite often I was asked why I wanted it. I said I wished to write to the gentleman. The next question was invariably, 'What was it with regard to?' I then replied loftily that I wished to make 'a certain suggestion to him'. I wasn't questioned further!

Along with the certain suggestion I enclosed the casket design and a typed selection of quotes from my letters approving the idea of 'over-the-counter coffins' and giving the address at which the originals could be inspected, in the time-honoured manner with unsolicited testimonials.

The answers were not long in arriving. All negative, which was not unexpected considering the novelty of the idea. Argos's and Sainsbury's replies were the most thoughtful and in the case of the latter really seemed to believe there was a future in such a project but not in their Homebase, House and Garden centres. I thought it particularly nice of them to write at such length, as I had mistakenly called Roy Griffiths Mister! Sorry, Sir.

So I was not too down-hearted. But it seemed that I was really 'into' funerals in a big way. Was it, I wondered,

for that reason that it seemed suddenly that the media
were too? Perhaps I just hadn't noticed before, but now
that I did, it seemed that funerals, and allied subjects,
were very much the in thing. There was the scandal of
the Westminster Council's sale of cemeteries for 15
pence; a report of an enterprising Yorkshireman, Edgar
Dakin, who, shocked at the prices charged for memorial
headstones in the conventional marble or granite, had
patented his design for thermoplastic ones at a tiny
fraction of the cost; and yet another that was virtually a
half-hour commercial on BBC television for the ubiqui-
tous Hodgson Holdings.

I learned a lot from other BBC programmes. I was
incensed by one on 'What to do if someone dies', in the
Advice Shop series, during which, in explaining the
procedure involved on registering a death, the narrator
said, 'The registrar will ask you what funeral director
you are using.' *Not* 'Are you using a funeral director?' I
wrote to say so and received a courteous reply from the
producer, who said, 'I'm interested in the DIY approach
you suggest and in our next series perhaps we'll look at
this more closely.' I do hope that they may.

Also Margo Macdonald in her *Ask Margo* series
explained more about arranging funerals.

From the two programmes I learned that, if cash is
really short, the DSS will pay for a funeral. A low-income
funeral, it appears, costs around £510. Without a grave it
costs £390/£400 (presumably this means cremation). A
grave costs an extra £120. (These prices were quoted in
February 1988). Here one meets with what I would deem
quite a drawback. The DSS will *not* pay for an 'individual'
grave, so a 'common' grave (that's with companions,
either already waiting or pending), is what you'll get. You
won't be allowed to erect a headstone, have a name-plate
or put flowers on a common grave, so is it any wonder
that the whole thing smacks of the dreaded 'pauper's
burial' and that, however poor, people will make
monumental sacrifices to raise the money somehow for
the 'something better' that they feel they should provide?

Unless ... unless they face the truth – the truth 'that will make ye free', according to the Bible – which in this case is that the love and/or respect that was earned by the deceased during their lifetime is there for ever in the minds and hearts of those who knew them. No amount of display or pomp is going to increase that, or lack of it detract.

And if I achieve nothing other than to make people realize that they have a choice if they wish to exercise it, I shall be satisfied.

5 Taboo Or Not Taboo

Recently I have been reading *Prick Up Your Ears*, the biography of Joe Orton by John Lahr. Orton, as we know, excelled in exposing the reflex thinking of contemporary society but it is not from Orton himself that I have cherished this quote, but from Alexander and Margarette Mitscherlich in *The Inability to Mourn*. It concerns taboo and is as follows: 'Whenever one dare not question any further or when it does not occur to one to do so, one is dealing with a taboo.' *Taboo exists to inhibit thought.*

And here is the immortal opening paragraph from *Winnie the Pooh*, A.A. Milne's eternal beloved teddy: 'Here is Edward Bear coming downstairs now, bump, bump, bump on the back of his head, behind Christopher Robin. It is, as far as he knows, the only way of coming downstairs, but sometimes he feels that there is really another way if only he could stop bumping for a moment and think of it.'

The bumping produced by taboo is subtler and more insidious than that felt by Pooh's head and, although painless, is just as potent in its power to inhibit thought. Habits of thinking *are* hard to break. It's so much easier to fall back on 'That's the way things are done' or 'It's the way I was brought up.' Put up a sign, 'No through road' and few will venture to ask 'Why?' or 'Are you sure?'

In one of the sketches in *Beyond the Fringe*, as I remember it, Jonathan Miller was a prisoner in the condemned cell, his execution scheduled for the next

morning. The warder in charge, plus the prison chaplain
and governor, both of whom visited him that night, talked
of anything and everything except the only event which
interested the condemned man. All the poor fellow wanted
to know was, 'Will it hurt?' This question was repeated
throughout the sketch and was parried every time. The
warder said, 'Oh, you don't want to think about that, sir.
What about a nice game of chess?' The chaplain said that it
didn't do to be morbid – a positive attitude was best all
round really. And the governor hoped he'd enjoyed his
dinner, 'Extra good tonight, wasn't it, my man. Have a
cigarette?' It was very funny and very revealing.

Somehow today death has become not quite a forbidden
topic but certainly a rather indecent one. To the medical
profession it means failure, and to the layman, as I
remarked earlier, a reminder of his mortality. Somehow
we don't want to think of death as a possibility, even in the
most inevitable circumstances. Clergy counselling on the
subject is rare nowadays. There are plenty of organi-
zations and support groups to turn to in bereavement, but
if there were more preparation, perhaps there would be
less need for reparation. I am, of course, here considering
only progressively fatal illnesses. With sudden deaths,
such as heart attacks and accidents, there can be no
preparation, and this is where, I'm sure, bereavement
counselling can benefit many.

But in any case, the mortal remains are an embarrassment. We put them away in a box or cover them with a
blanket as quickly as possible. Not so with animals. In
many parts of Britain, whole carcases hanging up in
markets and butchers' shops are not an unusual sight.
The other day I heard a story, allegedly true, of a child
who, observing this, asked his mother 'Where are the
people?' A bizarre and horrifying thought certainly in a
culture in which eating people is wrong, but one can
understand the child's question. I think it must be true.
Only a child could be so, as yet, untouched by the
conventions and taboos of our world.

Recently BBC Television showed a programme in the

Everyman series called *The Facts of Death*. It concerned the 'death education' programme which is now included in the curriculum in many schools throughout the United States. In describing the programme the *Radio Times* stated that, 'From Kindergarten to High School, children are being asked to face the facts of death. What should children be told and when?' Elizabeth Kubler-Ross, the 'death expert' I mentioned earlier, featured prominently and made her views clear, which are that, again quoting from the *Radio Times*, 'It's been estimated that by the time most American children reach their teens, they will have seen over 10,000 deaths in the cinema and on TV. But fiction puts a safe distance between the young and the realities of death. What's more, in the real world, the dead and dying are removed from the house to the antiseptic confines of a hospital and funeral home. As a result most young people know little about what the death of a loved one means.'

I watched the programme, which was most worthy in intent and expressed many of my own thoughts on the subject. Yet, as it progressed, I began to have doubts and felt a certain unease. Is it truly possible to prepare a child for death of a loved-one? Children are very immediate people, who nevertheless seem to be born with intimations of mortality. Rosencrantz, in Tom Stoppard's witty and wonderful play *Rosencrantz and Guildenstern Are Dead*, discourses thus on the subject:

Whatever became of the moment when one first knew about death? There must have been one, a moment in childhood, when it first occurred to you that you don't go on forever. It must have been shattering – stamped into one's memory. And you can't remember it. It never occurred to me at all. What does one make of that? We must be born with an intuition of mortality. Before we know the words for it, before we know there are words, out we come, bloodied and squalling with the knowledge that for all the compasses in the world, there's only one direction, and time is the only measure.

But death education? Teaching children to 'cope' with the death of a loved-one? Children are not small adults, except in the physical sense, and I would contend that this is well nigh impossible. It's a little like sex education, which I also have doubts about. Oh, well enough to explain about the mechanics of procreation; but feelings ...? Divorced from emotions, the sexual act appears, at best, to be a bit of a joke and at worst an incomprehensible assault. Sex education, at least to a child before puberty, is a tough class to take. They will be able to accept facts, but reactions will as a rule range from 'I should get the giggles if I had to do that' to 'I wouldn't let anyone do anything like that to me. It's disgusting!' I just wonder sometimes if it may do more harm than good. Luckily at a young age the whole thing seems as remote and improbable as, for instance, being grown up. Like finishing with school, which we are assured will happen one day but can't quite believe.

Much the same feeling of 'That's the kind of thing that happens to other people' must surely be the reaction to instruction in how to cope with the death of a loved-one. It's hard enough for adults. I would suggest that there aren't many of us who haven't felt that way after a bereavement. 'This is not the sort of thing that happens to me!' Followed by the eternal complaint of childhood, 'It's not fair!'

Also the death of a pet, to a child, can often be more upsetting than the death of, for example, a grandfather, however kind and nice. However fond the child may have been of him, a deeper bond often exists with the family cat who sleeps on his bed at night and who, if the experts are to be believed, plays a bigger part in the child's fantasies and dreams than any human. This was explored to some extent in the film. (I myself can remember losing all interest in the courageous rescues of shipwrecked sailors by the lifeboat off the coast of Northumberland, when I realized it was rowed by a mere woman – Grace Darling, and not by a grey starling!'

The thought of the death of a parent or sibling *seemed*

to be accepted with a certain equanimity, simply, I would think, because such a thing is unimaginable. The children who had actually experienced this and spoke of their feelings said that their rage and feeling of total betrayal at such a time were denied expression, that they were discouraged from 'dwelling' on it and felt guilty about their feelings of deep resentment. With the best intentions, the grown-ups do their best to distract the child in order that he will more quickly forget. Sadly the intentions backfire. The child needs help to talk the bitterness out of his system. This is what bereavement counselling is all about, and it is quite a different thing from death education.

Nowadays we are encouraged to absorb more information about other lives, institutions and professions than ever before. Facts are poured over us relentlessly by the media. On television we are surfeited with operations on, and in, the most private and intimate parts of our bodies. We watch the delivery of babies, and it's hard now to remember how short a time it is since that was first shown to the viewing public.

I can imagine the soul-searching, endless meetings and breast-banging that went on before such an item was first given the go-ahead to be screened, because, as we know, birth and particularly gestation were taboo subjects until well into the twentieth century. Women literally stayed at home when they could no longer disguise the fact that, barring accidents, they would shortly be adding to the population statistics. Now they carry all before them with pride; ships in full sail parading in every high street. Conversely, breast feeding, which was once carried out wherever and whenever demanded (except in the higher echelons of society, where ladies usually employed a wet-nurse so that their social life was not disrupted) is now a private activity. Although the actual display of the mammaries is becoming more frequent and acceptable, the lady prefers to withdraw when using them for the purpose for which they were designed.

The Victorians were less unaccustomed to death than we. Owing to the defectiveness of drains and the prevalence of draughts, there was more of it about. The deathbed scene was popular; few novels or dramas were complete without at least one. Not that I am suggesting that the romanticizing of death is in any way preferable to the sanitization of it, but for some reason it seems that the shibboleths of our society, at any given time, demand either one or the other.

However, one type of death which seems always to have been acceptable, indeed expected, is the 'Bang! Bang!' – or earlier, the 'Stab! Stab!' – 'You're dead!' variety; from *Hamlet*, which certainly had its share, even discounting 'poor Yorick', to the present-day Westerns and Bond films. This is the glamorization of death, with no consequences to the victim: no orphaned children, grieving widows or anxiety about future livelihood in the absence of the breadwinner. This kind of death strikes no kind of horror, even among the recently bereaved; indeed, the films are often referred to as 'escapist' entertainment. I suppose they do no harm. They do, however, point up our ambivalence towards the whole subject and explain, to some extent, the death-education programme in the States.

In contrast, television news programmes seldom show close-ups of the bodies of white victims of accident or violence, by either man or nature. I do not imply that this is a racist distinction but simply that in the 'civilized' world when a person becomes a corpse they are covered with a sheet before you can say 'Not in front of the children.'

But is it really the children's sensibilities we are protecting? I think not. Dead pigs – dead people. 'Oh, look, Mummy – that poor lion hasn't got a Christian!' – again underlining the point that the child identifies more completely with the animal than the human. No, it's our own rejection of death which will also finally prevent their chance of developing a less blinkered view than their parents.

We are bombarded with facts; we are taken over nuclear and hydro-electic power stations, we visit slate mines and are escorted down fruit and vegetable production lines by enthusiastic or disapproving presenters. Documentaries about mental institutions and prisons are becoming commonplace; windmills, watermills and sewage works all come under close scrutiny. Most we can see on the box as well as visit in person, hear about on the box as well as visit in person, hear about on the radio and read about in books. Is there nothing we can't see or hear?

When referring to the hanging carcases, I was careful to say that this practice can be seen still in many parts of Britain. Not all. As the prudery regarding death seems to spread with the growth of affluence and religious doubts, so in the home counties there is a greater demand for insulation from the unpleasant facts of life – and death, and such displays are rarer. Our hypocrisy is finally nailed by the fact that, to my knowledge, there has, to date, been no television documentary on a day in the death at your friendly neighbourhood slaughter-house (sorry – abattoir; French words always sound so much daintier, don't they?). We watch veterinary surgeons making animals better but not slaughterers making them corpses. We see cows; we eat steak. What we don't want to see is how one becomes the other. We prefer to buy it neatly packaged, disguised into shapes nature never designed; displayed in a cold cabinet and decorated with plastic parsley and red peppers, rather than have our requirement hacked off and wrapped in newspaper by a man in a bloody apron, from a traditional butcher's slab.

In *A Sideways Look*, broadcast on 18 December 1987, that inestimable broadcaster Anthony Smith put it thus:

> Most of us steadfastly eat meat, and we therefore approve of slaughter houses, so what kind of hypocrites are we that we never got to see them? And would hate even to see a picture of one, say, in our own newspaper at the

up-graded slaughter time of Christmas. Or to put that question the other way round, would we change our meat eating habits if we had to see, just once in a lifetime, where our meat came from, and how it came, and what the place smelt like, and what else had to be done before, in its neat plastic wrapping, it is there on the supermarket shelves. My suspicion is that vegetarianism would gain recruits by the thousand, by the million.

Denis Nilson, the mass murderer of Muswell Hill, created a disgusted outcry, such as that accorded to all such criminals, but to a far greater extent. The reason was his dismembering of his victims after the crime. This was reported to Nilson, who remarked that, in his opinion, Society had got its priorities a bit cock-eyed. It is not surprising that he refused to plead insanity!

So back to the child and his question. 'Oh! well, the people, dear – well, the people – go to the parlour – that's what it's called, you see – the funeral parlour; resting; in a chapel meant just for them to do it in. What do you mean, do what in? Rest, of course. No! Of course they don't live there for ever. They go to another place. No, not heaven, that's later – Oh do shut up!'

It's not easy, of course, to explain about death to a child, particularly if we ourselves find it embarrassing. The child's total matter-of-factness can be disconcerting. Friends in the Netherlands thought they were doing frightfully well with their 6-year-old whose 5-month-old kitten had been run over. The abject motorist brought the little creature in. The parents explained that, sadly, the animal would never get any better and would be unable to run about and play any more, ever. The child listened carefully while regretting the dead kitten and then said, 'Well, in that case he'd better go and live somewhere else!'

In the words of Scarlett O'Hara, 'I'll think about that tomorrow.' That seems the usual attitude and, of course, no one would suggest a morbid preoccupation with death to be anything but unhealthy. But I was forty-two before

I saw a dead body, and surely there's something wrong with having been so insulated from such a natural and frequent occurrence?

However, this illusion of immortality is no bad thing in our day-to-day lives; it helps us to get through them. People who lose it temporarily, due to their suffering from what is now known as the 'post-trauma shock syndrome' – the King's Cross fire, the *Herald of Free Enterprise* and the Lockerbie Boeing crash are well-known examples – become apprehensive, often fearing to go out for a time. Possibly never again venturing into lifts, subways or cable cars and refusing to look down from high places.

Our attempts to deny death seem to me to be connected in some way with our worship of youth. the thought of ageing is uncomfortable – particularly middle-ageing, when one realizes one is further from birth and nearer to the Never, Never Land. Everyone wants to live a long time but nobody wants to be old; but as Dad was told by Mother, you can't have one without etc, etc. I mean, we all have to get old or die in the attempt!

Also, in our present acquisitive culture, death represents the loss not merely of living but also of having and of buying. It is possible that a life (death) without our Saturday shopping spree in B & Q is unthinkable and therefore unfaced.

One of the superstores I approached with my suggestion of flat-pack coffins replied that, although interested, they didn't think it was for them, as they believed that DIY home improvement is a leisure activity based on the future and, therefore, not associated with death, and so it would not fit in with the family shopping trip, which they seek to encourage. Well ...! Apart from the fact that death is the only real certainty in anyone's future, I wondered, as the duration of that future contracts, at what age would Grannie and Grandpa become less welcome for family shopping?

This, I know, is carping. I was grateful to those managing and marketing directors who gave serious consideration to my proposals, and to those who didn't trouble to reply or replied in two lines baldly stating that they were not interested – pity! I think they'll be made to eat their words within a very few years.

An admission that the cost of funerals is causing growing alarm would appear to be endorsed by the ever-increasing number of advertisements appearing for dying on the instalment plan and 'pay now die later' schemes. The Co-op are offering an added inducement of vouchers to spend in their shops on anything except food. The exclusion is not explained!

There seems every probability that the funeral tycoons are going to have a bonanza in about fifteen years from now, because the first antibiotic generation will all be moving on within a year or two of each other. The big operators must be rubbing their hands.

I decided it was time to find out a bit more about quite a lot of things.

6 Finding Out

Well, how? For a start I decided to write again to the gentleman in Hornchurch whom I quoted earlier, who said in his letter, after hearing the broadcast, that he had had three very distressing experiences at family funerals due to the services provided by those presiding over them. Three sounded a bit excessive, and I asked him if he would be prepared to let me have further details. This he kindly did, and at length, so I hope he will forgive me if I abbreviate them somewhat. He wrote:

> The first was at my sister's funeral where the Anglican minister arrived late at the crematorium. The hearse had been brought to the entrance and the coffin lifted onto the bearers but they, and the party of mourners, were not allowed into the chapel. No one knew why, and no explanation was offered by the crematorium authorities until after the ceremony and then just a bald statement that the minister was late. When at last the service got under way the Minister described my sister as having been a good mother. She had no children. Other references made were not in the least relevant to her life or personality. This greatly distressed all close relations; my mother, another sister and the widower were of course present.
>
> The second disappointment was at that of my mother, to whom I was very close. With my sister's funeral in mind, I spent thirty minutes with the minister who was to

take the service (he had been appointed by the funeral director). I had chosen two hymns – one of which seemed very fitting – but the Minister objected to it as apparently it was a Methodist hymn! I told him of my mother's life, her great character, courage, love and energy, and how she had worked for her family in very difficult times and how, in return, she was dearly loved by them and her friends; I said that I wanted these feelings expressed in the service, plus our pride in our mother and all she had done and sacrificed for us. I mentioned her hobbies, etc. and that she had attended regularly a social club for pensioners held in a local church. It was only then that he seemed to show any interest which subsided when he learned that it was the church opposite his which was Roman Catholic!

However I thought that all was clear regarding the service. I should have known better, as he had not made one single note, not even the name that everyone knew her by, i.e. Sally. She had been christened Sarah Stroud. During the service, each time he mentioned my mother it was as Sarah Stroud Smith and not one word of our previous discussion or my requests. It was just the usual preachings about the love of God and sinners, etc. and had no relevance to parting with a beloved mother, grandmother and friend. It was just another event to him, a factory line service, totally lacking any personal reference to the deceased or the bereaved. That disappointment will always be with me; I felt ashamed – that I had let my mum down; something she had never done to me. It seemed our last chance to express our feelings; a moment in time never to be repeated; and the chance was lost. I will never forget it or get over it.

Later I complained strongly to the Crematorium, the funeral director, the Minister, his Bishop and to Lambeth Palace. I had meetings with all these people and although they were sympathetic I was left feeling that nothing would be done to make funeral services a more personal affair.

I have quoted this second example of my Hornchurch friend's experience at some length as I feel it epitomizes many of the complaints expressed to me, i.e. the impersonal, factory conveyor-belt approach. My heart goes out to him and all others who have experienced similar disappointments. Also I cannot help comparing these uninspiring ceremonies with the way we said goodbye to Nigel, and feel renewed gratitude that somewhere in my make-up is the stubborn gene that gave me the determination to do it my way. I feel sorry too for the ministers who deliver these arid addresses. What a missed opportunity perhaps to gather some not-too-regular worshippers into their fold. At such a time mourners would often be ripe for conversion by a minister who conducted a concerned, personal and warmly human service.

The third incident involved my correspondent's wife's family at the funeral of her grandmother. He writes:

It was a Jewish cemetery – the first Jewish funeral I had attended. According to the usual ritual, the non-Jewish people were separated from the Jewish in an entrance room, awaiting the arrival of the coffin from another building. As soon as it appeared there was a very quick prayer, and we all followed the coffin, which was being pushed on a trolley to the grave. The grave digger had piled the earth all round it making it impossible to get near. It was pouring with rain and the mourners had to stand on the path alongside other recently dug graves. It reminded me of a Hammer Horror movie.

We then returned to the little waiting room where further prayers in Hebrew took place at great speed. It was an embarrassingly short service and at such a pace that everyone was upset, particularly my mother-in-law, who was in great distress. I then found out that the Rabbi had decided to cut it short and take it at speed because eight Jewish males were not present among the mourners. The Jewish people present were disgusted. They had not been advised in advance that such was necessary and they expected, and had paid for, the full service. To be let down and embarrassed at such a time seemed unforgivable. Who do these so called Priests – representatives of God – think they are? It puts religion in a very bad light and their attitudes to death are disrespectful and lacking in the understanding that would help people to bear their grief better and with pride.

He continues: 'I took up the cause of flat pack coffins and wrote to the Sales Directors of Magnet and Southern, MFI and Texas and did not receive a reply from any of them.'

Next I returned to my original source – the booklet *It's a R.I.P. Off*, and in particular to Richard Buckley, the retired funeral director whose words of wisdom started it all for me. He states: 'The funeral business today *is* a business. The whole idea is to make as much money as possible. All the sympathy and that sort of thing is a load of pseudo old rubbish.'

I decided to telephone this outspoken gentleman, who has turned out to be a constant source of information and amusement to me ever since. Always willing to chat, it's easy to be sidetracked by his great fund of knowledge from the '...old days, when there was a certain amount of respect shown to the local undertaker. Nowadays you go into a pub and they take the rise out of you.' Perhaps this is not too surprising! He told me also of the habit of undertakers, if they hadn't been paid on time, of sending the hearse, complete with black horses with their purple plumes, to stand outside the door of the debtor, thereby letting the whole street know that the bill had not yet been paid. *But* this was only in the case of a basic minimum funeral, i.e. costing around £10. For a £50 one (a great deal of money in those days) the account was never pushed for and could take years to settle.

It was also news to me that no kind of licence is required to set up as an undertaker. 'You just put up a plate and get on with it.'

It was Richard Buckley also who wrote, 'Every funeral director in some respects pays for his own work. If he doesn't offer an inducement to the coroner's officers, it will be to the mortuary keepers, masons, nurses in private nursing homes or wardens of old people's homes. It's rife throughout the trade and always had been.'

The trade seems to have lost none of its competitive spirit since an undertaker named Strowgen invented the very first automatic telephone exchange to stop operators intercepting his business and tipping off a rival firm.

Having interviewed several funeral directors by telephone and personally, under the auspices of the BBC for the *Punters* programme, I nevertheless, when shopping in a nearby town, decided to try one more. I asked the cost of their cheapest funeral. This was £280 and included:

A veneered chipboard coffin

Handles, name-plate and lining

Bearers

Hearse

Transport from place of death to funeral parlour (if ten miles or less) and to cemetery or crematorium (also if ten miles or less).

Doctors' certificates – I had specified cremation – and crematorium fees brought the total cost up to £360.

The following conversation then ensued between the funeral director and me:

Me: Can you itemize the basic funeral components for me?

F.D.: No, that is our block charge for a simple basic funeral.

Me: I would like my own friends and relations to act as bearers. Would you have any objection?

F.D: No, none at all.

Me: By how much would that reduce the cost?

F.D.: Not at all, I'm afraid. This is a basic charge system and follows a similar pattern to that used by most funeral directors.

Me: You mean if we, the family, brought the deceased
           to your premises to await disposal, there would be
           no reduction?

F.D.:   I'm afraid not. [By this time he sensed that I was
           shopping around and said:] You won't find
           anything cheaper in this area.

Me: Yes, I think that's probably true unless we do it
           ourselves.

F.D.:   Oh you can't do that!

Me: Why?

F.D.:   Well, you'd have to make a coffin for one thing.

Me: Unless I purchased one from a funeral directors'
           suppliers?

F.D.:   You couldn't do that.

Me: Why?

F.D.:   They wouldn't sell you one.

Me: Why?

F.D.:   I don't know.

Me: Could it be that firms like yours would be down on
           them like a ton of bricks if they dared to sell a
           coffin retail?

F.D.:   (very uncomfortable): Perhaps.

Now he was a nice man, and I apologize to him in case
he ever reads this; he had his orders. Nevertheless, I
happen to know that coffin-bearers, for instance, are paid
around £5 per funeral and that either four or six are
used, depending on the weight of the coffin and its
occupant. So why no reduction?

I did manage to extract from him the cost to the
customer of the coffin included in the basic charge,
which, he said, was £78, but had absolutely no luck in
getting him to give me a breakdown of the items making
up the remaining £200.

Such itemization is now law in many states of North
America, along with the stipulation that prices must be
quoted over the telephone if requested. In our market
forces orientated society this should be mandatory. MPs
please take note. And while on the subject of legislation,
'The Dignity in Death Alliance', which represents nearly

fifty charities and pensioners' groups, might like, instead
of supporting 'pay now – die later' schemes, to press the
government to follow the Swiss example. There, a simple,
basic funeral is the right of every citizen. The attitude of
the Swiss authorities seems very logical as well as
civilized, recognizing that death, like birth, of which it is
the inevitable consequence, is similarly unavoidable by
the individual concerned.

The Central Television programme in which I took
part included an interview with a spokesman for the
National Funeral Directors Association, one Mr Geoffrey
White, which contained the following statement: 'A
funeral is something that you do only once. If you are
tiling your bathroom and get it wrong, you can always
scrape it off and start again. You can't do that with a
funeral. If you get it wrong you're stuck with that
memory for the rest of your life.' And if the funeral
director gets it wrong, you'll nevertheless get a hefty bill
into the bargain! He goes on to say, 'If people want to
have a go at doing it themselves we've got nothing to stop
them.' There was a somewhat rueful tone in this. 'But I
would remind them it's a once only episode. If they do get
it wrong they'll live with that memory forever.'

However, reports of recent cases in the United States
show that funeral directors don't always get it right and
that much misery can be caused by the results. *The
Funeral Service Journal* of August 1988 reports two
recent cases in the States, the first of which entailed a
funeral home which was a front for a drug ring; even
more alarming is a report in the *Wolverhampton Express
and Star* of a funeral director in Florida who was
arrested for failing to perform funerals for which he had
been paid. The news item states: 'Inspectors earlier in
the month had found forty bodies stacked in closets and
the cremated remains of twenty-six people. This macabre
discovery was made at the "Morning Glory" funeral home
in Jacksonville which was owned by a Mr Howell.'

Mr Howell is accused of grand theft for taking $5,500
for unperformed burials and cremations, and faces
thirty-six charges of fraud and other misconduct,

including failure to embalm or refrigerate bodies. One body had been at the home since November 1978, another since April 1979 and others from 1980 and 1981. These charges refer to the remains of sixty-seven bodies.

The exploits of Burke and Hare seem almost to be relegated into the realms of mythology. Apparently this is not so. In the late summer of 1989 three members of a family named Sconce, mother, father and son, faced trial in Pasadena on sixty-seven criminal counts. These included the multiple cremations of human remains after the unlawful removal of parts of the bodies. It was stated that it was their habit to remove and sell parts of the dead. The lawyer who is representing more than a hundred families who are suing the Sconces' funeral home has offered a $50,000 reward for information which will lead to the conviction of others responsible for illegally selling body parts. He stated that corneas sold for $565, heads for $85 and kidneys and spleens for up to $300. He added that this was, 'an Auschwitz-type operation, with pure profit as its only motive'. It appears that medical schools bought more than half the body parts. Does this, I wonder, imply that the other half were sold – to whom? Further profit, it was alleged, was made from the theft of gold and silver extracted from teeth. The attorney representing the families of the desecrated deceased said that the advertisement and reward were aimed at encouraging workers in the industry to come forward with information that he said could expose what was now a multi-million-dollar industry.

Nearer home, the *Enfield Independent* of 24 August 1988, reported that a funeral director – by name Seaward & Sons – came considerably unstuck when a funeral cortège under their auspices failed to arrive at the home of the deceased to pick up the mourners. It transpired later that the body of Mrs Lilian Kelly, who had left instructions that she wished to be buried next to her husband, had actually been cremated the day before! The managing director, Mr Pat Webb, is quoted as saying, 'The only comment I can possibly make is that the mistake was absolutely genuine. [!?] A human error was made by a member of my staff and he will be disciplined.'

One would like to know if the mourners at the previous day's cremation had realized that they were seeing off a foreign body, and what happened to the body, if any, that should have been disposed of that day? Also, who paid for what? The mind reels at the thought of such permutations.

And what about cryonics? Cry what? ONICS. Unless you caught the BBC *Everyman* programme *The Immortalists*, it would not be surprising if the word was unknown to you; but make no mistake, there is a hard sell going on at the moment from the United States to try to persuade funeral directors in Britain to take up this futuristic notion. In the most simple terms, it is a process whereby freshly dead remains are preserved until such time when science and technology have reached a point whereby they can be reanimated and restored to 'a youthful and perpetual life'.

Yes, I'm not kidding, nor, incidentally, am I knocking the idea. It might be lovely. On the other hand, it would depend how long one would have to stay in this state of suspended animation. I mean, suppose it were fifty years; when resuscitated, one wouldn't know anybody. It's a pity there are no first-hand reports in existence of R.V. Winkle's reactions. No roving reporter to ask, 'How does it feel, Mr Winkle, to be suddenly restored to your conscious state after one hundred years?' And even if it were a much shorter period, no one would know *you* if you had died around the three-score-and-ten mark and came to life again all sprauncy and seventeen! I think it might be preferable, after all, for the dear, old-fashioned scientists to carry on in their determination to 'prolong active life' for us humans as well as our dogs.

The Independent Order of Odd Fellows publishes a periodic review of funeral costs. The 1986 edition contained the results of a survey conducted the previous year. Three hundred questionnaires were dispatched to

funeral directors throughout the country. Only ten per
cent replied. Some had been requested by the National
Association of Funeral Directors Public Relations Officer
to refer this survey to head office and, 'Please contact
National Office, London. We understand that the
Association's Public Relations Consultants are in
possession of most of the statistics you require.' The
statistical information, relating as it did specifically to
'the cost of your last two funerals', could not be available
centrally, nor could the funeral directors' opinions which
were being sought.

The 1990 review undertaken by the same society
showed the average costs for a simple funeral, including
necessary disbursements was £920 for a burial and £712
for cremation. Broken down into regions, burials were
most expensive in East Anglia and cremations in South
Wales. To obtain a copy of this latest leaflet, which
contains a great deal more relevant information, send a
SAE to the Order of Odd Fellows (address on p.174).

A news item worthy of note taken from the same
pamphlet states that in Portsmouth a local showman's
funeral involved three funeral directors, eight coffin-
bearers, five coachloads of mourners and a hermetically
sealed coffin in twenty-gauge steel-and-pewter finish
from America, making a total cost of £2,472. This sum
did not include the floral tributes.

At this point I would like to make it clear that when
Nigel and I discussed DIY funerals, it was not because we
had anything against either undertakers or ministers of
religion. We had just considered them an unnecessary
expense and superfluous to our requirements. I was truly
unprepared for the reaction of the public to the *Punters*
broadcast which uncovered such a wave of resentment
and hostility.

But if there are people who were satisfied with the
funerals provided and who considered that they had
received good value for money, I wish that they too had
written and told me so. Perhaps there were others who
were even surprised by the warmth and humanity of the

funeral director and minister concerned, and I wish that
they had done likewise. After all, it is usually an attack
on a proposition that generates the greatest correspondence. But not in this case.

I read recently of a funeral director who started his
business in 1952 and was ordained as a priest in 1983.
The Revd. Reg Harvey said that the combined roles of
priest and undertaker fit in well together, particularly in
the 'pastoral matter of care of the bereaved'. I'm sure
they do, and equally sure that temporal matters are not
neglected either, as it would surely take very determined
mourners to arrange for the disposal of the deceased with
a rival firm! Perhaps the profession as a whole, who have
recently been complaining of a drop in business, might
like to consider this innovation.

Just recently I received my monthly copy of *Funeral
Service Journal*, to which I subscribe.

In one issue I placed an advertisement which read:
'Funeral directors or suppliers willing to supply coffins to
general public please contact Jane Spottiswoode for
inclusion in her forthcoming book *Undertaken with Love*.
Any answers to be sent to [box number].' More than two
months went by without response, which didn't wholly
surprise me. Then I received an answer from an
undertaking firm in Blackburn, from a Mr James Gibson.
He said that he was willing not only to supply coffins but
to arrange transport if required. I gladly pass on the
address of this gentleman, to whom I am deeply grateful.
It is Gibsons Funeral Undertakers, 134 Darwen Street,
Blackburn, Lancs. Telephone Blackburn 681500 and also
Bolton 655869. His coffins range from £45, for the
cheapest, including handles and screws, to around £300
for solid oak.

It is not the first time that I have had reason to be
indebted to this admirable journal, it being entirely
independent. It proved that by devoting a whole page to
the story of my efforts to dispose of Nigel in the way we
both wanted – complete with a photograph of me sitting
on my coffin in the loft; I felt I had reached the zenith of

all publicity on the subject!

A few pages on and it seems as though my arrangements even had the approval of the professionals. In an article headed 'Death, the unresolved mystery of life', a lady named Georgia Bange, of the Colonial Funeral Home, Leesburg, Virginia, concludes with the words, 'Once we cross the hurdle of accepting death as a fact of life, we can then begin to make ourselves knowledgeable concerning the needs of others in regard to the death of a loved one and [this is the bit I like] the therapeutic value of being involved with the funeral and final rites of a loved one.'

Could Ms Bange have meant that? Would she really endorse a DIY funeral, thereby doing herself out of a job? If so, this total altruism in our materialistic universe is indeed 'other-worldly'. But I cannot believe that she really wanted her words to be interpreted quite so literally!

So far, so negative. In the next chapter I will try to offer some practical and positive advice and tell something about how one can avoid the professionals, as I did.

7 Doing It Yourself

In her preface to *The American Way of Death*, Jessica Mitford said that, when she started on the book, some of her friends and advisers were frankly appalled at her choice of subject. Things haven't changed much. So were some of mine; but, I'm happy to say, not too many. Most were encouraging, and they will have my eternal gratitude.

When asked by the BBC interviewer whether he thought more people ought to get involved in DIY funerals, Alan replied; 'Yes, but ... provided they have the benefit of someone else's experience. Not everyone has the right conditions for a learning experience such as we've had.' I would endorse that one hundred per cent and add one or two provisos of my own:

1. If it has been well discussed in a family situation and both the individual and the next of kin are determined on it, thereby ensuring that it is well planned ahead of time.

2. If the logistics have been thoroughly considered. Remember also that, although a coffin by itself is not a great weight and fairly easy to manoeuvre when in an upright position, you should give some thought to the time when it will be horizontal and heavier, and make sure that as an amateur you can cope.

3. If with the planning and the execution you take it one step at a time. It will work if you really want it to, but always remember that if, for any reason, you decide to change your mind at any time and wish to proceed

through the usual channels, i.e. call in a funeral director, you can still do so. He will not refuse your money!

4. If you possibly can, try to have friends like mine!

Something that started out as a personal endeavour has become not only a campaign but also a quest. I say 'quest' because I would hate anyone to regard this book as the definitive guide to DIY funerals, and I cannot emphasize this too strongly. There is much I still don't know, and information is far from easy to come by. The funeral directors' lobby is very strong and, although not a closed shop (as I pointed out earlier, anyone can do it), it thrives upon the closed mind and regards any request for knowledge as the greatest impertinence.

Looking back, it amazes me that we managed as well as we did. The essentials are:

A coffin.

A death certificate from a doctor (two doctors if cremation is chosen).

The Registration of Death certificate, which must be in the hands of the crematorium or cemetery authorities before the funeral takes place.

A station wagon or hatchback, roomy enough to take the coffin.

In my case the letter from the British Humanist Association and the knowledge that, as next of kin, I actually *owned* my husband's body (and provided I did nothing to contravene the Environmental Health Act, my decision with regard to his disposal was final) were a great comfort and relief.

Information on the documentation required and formalities to be complied with can be found in *What To Do When Someone Dies*, published by the Consumers Association. Also therein is a useful chart of the order in which to cope with this. It looks formidable, but that is because it takes into account so many types and locations of death. Striking out all that does not apply to you greatly simplifies the procedure.

The same publication gives advice on another formality which in the past was invested with much mystique but is really quite simple. That is the 'laying-out', also known as 'the last offices'. The family can under-take it themselves if wished, or employ a district nurse if they prefer. But it must be done fairly soon after death. It consists of laying the body on the back, closing the eyes and tying the jaw with a light bandage. Then washing, and in the case of a man, shaving, combing the hair and dressing in whatever clothing is wished. A clean nightdress or shirt is most usual nowadays. The natural outlets of the body used to be plugged with cotton wool but this, hospitals tells me, is no longer done except in the rare occasions of a conti-nuing discharge of body fluids after death. If the body is to be kept at home, it is advisable that the room be kept as cool as possible.

If the death takes place in hospital, the family and friends will have to collect the body. This will mean taking the coffin there, and it would also be useful to take a body bag which is leakproof and entirely enclosed. I have purchased mine from Lear of London (address on p.174). It cost £15.85 plus VAT (yes, really) of £2.38 and postage at £4. The postage seems excessive but it was a minimum price. Again, as with the coffin, I imagine that an individual order is not common. Some hospitals will keep the body in cold storage in their mortuary for a few days until the funeral can take place.

As funeral directors charge by mileage, most people choose a cemetery or crematorium near their home. At present most of these are still owned by local authorities. A telephone call will tell you their current fees and other details necessary to attend to. The DIYer is freer in his choice. So shop around (or get a friend or relation to oblige) and sort one out. I took the nearest, and as I have said, it was a beautiful site and the staff were helpful and efficient, and no obstacles were put in our way. Nigel was carried down the aisle by his human bearers, whereas in many crematoria they insist that a trolley takeover at the door to deliver the deceased to the catafalque. This should be checked on as well if it is important to you.

Not being a church-goer, I have no idea how the

ministers of the many religions practised in Britain
would feel if requested to officiate at a DIY funeral by a
member of their flock. I suppose their reactions would be
as varied as most people's are on most subjects, but the
findings of a survey would make an interesting read.

I would strongly advise having the coffin ready,
whether it is bought from a supplier or made by a
carpenter. As I have explained, I had a loft, which was a
great help, but it can be stored in a shed or garage.
Familiarity will disperse all the usual unpleasant
associations. The design of a rectangular casket type,
already referred to, would make a splendid blanket box.
Try to think of it as such – just a wooden box, that's all it
is. You'll be surprised how soon it will become an
accepted piece of household furniture. With a padded top
to match your curtains, it would make an attractive
window-seat-cum-storage-unit. Don't think I'm not
aware that this sounds like one of those hilarious
monologues performed by the late Joyce Grenfell, but if
you still feel this after enjoying the giggle, I think that
possibly a DIY funeral is not for you, because I'm dead
(sorry) serious.

A quite excellent fact sheet which I most strongly
recommend you get is published by Age Concern. It can
be obtained from them by writing to that organization.
(You will find their address on p.173.) This leaflet is
simply written and easy to understand and *does* contain
information regarding planning a funeral without the
use of a funeral director. I have only one quarrel with the
compilers. It is stated that, 'Some funeral directors will
assist in do-it-yourself funerals by supplying a simple
coffin and dealing with the documentation.' Where are
these philanthropists, Mr Gibson apart, I wonder? I'd love
to hear from them. They seem a bit thin on the ground in
these parts. In its list of useful publications this fact sheet
also includes the BBC booklet which was so valuable to
me, *It's a R.I.P. Off*, which has been out of print for some
time. Perhaps there'll be another programme along the
same lines, and an updated booklet. It would certainly be

very useful.

Many people hoping to save cost and trouble will their bodies to medical research and think no more about it. This often bequeaths more worries than assistance to the next-of-kin or whoever is arranging the funeral. As I mentioned in Chapter 1, it depends partly on the cause of death. The list of those unacceptable grows all the time and now includes AIDS as well as cancer, accident victims and anyone who has undergone a post-mortem examination. Up-to-date information can be obtained from HM Inspector of Anatomy (whose address is on p.173). He will know if there is a teaching hospital willing to accept you. Swift action must obviously be taken on death to inform him. Afterwards the medical school will arrange and pay for a funeral, and the family can attend if they wish.

It must be well known by now also that many people donate organs for transplanting, and many operations are being held up because of shortages. Hearts, livers and kidneys can save lives, and corneas can save sight. Either a donor card must have been signed by the deceased or no objections be made by the relations, when asked. Again, not all patients are suitable as donors. The decision will still rest with the doctors concerned. Removal must take place very soon after death and takes only a few hours. Afterwards the body is returned to the relations, and in this case the funeral expenses will not be paid by the hospital.

Burial on one's own land is perfectly legal and could save a lot of trouble and some money. For one thing, unless you wanted one, you wouldn't need a coffin. The local authority must be consulted and will want to know, among other things, that the depth of the grave complies with the regulations. Also tell the Water Board of your plans, as it would obviously not be a good idea to choose a site over, or near, an underground stream. In addition, one has just as much security of tenure there as in any churchyard. The Church of England has always reserved the right to dig you up again and redevelop the site in any way it chooses. (One can imagine the tasteful flashing neon sign of the St John of the Cross Rollarena or Bingo Palace.)

Burial at sea is a method favoured by some, but it counts as removal out of the country, and therefore the coroner must be notified and his acknowledgement received. Permission must also be granted by the inspectorate of fisheries; the address of your local one will be supplied by the Fisheries Inspectorate, MAFF, Great Westminster House, Horseferry Road, London, SW1P 2AE. If you decide to use a coffin, it has to be weighed down and have holes drilled in it to be certain it will sink. It is also sensibly specified that the weights must be of a material that will not harm fish. Nevertheless, it is stated that a shroud is preferred.

I hope that by now I have convinced at least some readers that a DIY funeral shouldn't be too hard to set up and certainly cheaper than can be had from the professionals.

As to costs, well, mine were as follows:

Coffin	£41.97
Crematorium fee, including box for ashes	£105.00
Fees for doctors who signed death certificates	£45.00
	£191.97

A simple short announcement in a national newspaper cost me £31.63, making a total cost of £223.60.

Of course, if Nigel hadn't died on a Thursday before a bank holiday weekend and had gone to the crematorium chapel as arranged by Alan, this would have incurred an additional cost of £60, i.e. £10 per night. In these parts you can still get bed and breakfast, in simple but comfortable style, for that price, but it seems that everything costs more if you're dead. Even, I'm told, the flowers.

All the present fal-lal has been slowly developing over
the last 200 years. Before then, undertaking was not a
trade. A local carpenter made the coffin if you yourself
didn't have the skill, and the rest was up to friends and
relations. The deceased stayed at home until the funeral
– 'the body vanishes' being a comparatively new
phenomenon. There's a lot of talk these days about
getting back to one's roots, and if I felt the slightest need
to justify what I did, which I don't, I could point out that
that was exactly what I'd done.

A BBC interviewer asked me if the making of the
programme about Nigel's funeral had been painful in the
memories it recalled. I said that on the contrary it had
acted as a catharsis. I would say the same of the writing
of this book and, in addition, if it gives its readers a
different viewpoint on death and disposal will be an added
satisfaction.

Unlike so many worthwhile campaigns, this one needs
no change in the law of the land, only a change in the
minds and attitudes of the people who live in it. There is
growing support in many ways, from many different
points of view; all over the country hardy, independent
spirits are fighting in their own corners in their own way,
and all of us for the same ends – for the freedom of choice,
which is ours by right, to be made easier to exercise.

There is Steve Nicholson in his DIY shop 'Timberman'
in Gainsborough, Lincs, who for two years supplied
coffins direct to the public offering ready-built ones or the
flat-pack self-assembly type for as little as £56. He also
offered a country-wide delivery service. However, after
achieving a certain amount of publicity Mr Nicholson's
suppliers were unable to supply him further and sadly he
can no longer offer this facility.

I very much liked the name of his service which was
'Sepulti' and his motto which means 'I did the best I could'.
Ironic considering the, perhaps, inevitable outcome.

And Edgar Dakin, who, shocked by a report that people
in the Welsh Valleys, unable to meet the stonemasons'
monumental costs, were burying their dead under

home-made wooden crosses, came up with a most practical and economic answer. He designed a memorial made of thermoplastic which can be produced at a tenth of the cost of a conventional headstone. He holds a patent and is waiting for sponsorship from some far-sighted entrepreneur.

His memorials, he maintains, will withstand wind and weather, and when a family grave is purchased, it would seem that his invention really comes into its own. It has on it the name of the first member of the family to die, and below three or more pull-out blanks. The idea is that when the next member of the family dies, instead of having to lift it (a marble or granite equivalent would weigh around three hundredweight), in order to have the next name added, you merely pull out the next blank and put in the new name. This, he states, will cost £120 for a family of four. But his imagination doesn't stop there. He can also make one for family pets which, if he can get it onto the market, will enable him to finance his human monuments. At £30 I have a feeling this could take off and make a healthy profit in this country of pet-lovers. I wish him well.

The all-too-common conveyor-belt system of disposals combined with falling church membership has encouraged secular societies in offering a more personal ceremony – they don't call them services – which celebrate the life of the departed rather than anticipating one to come.

Secular funerals were pioneered by the early free-thought societies and are now conducted by officiants of the Humanist Association and the National Secular Society. Traditionally it has been only out-and-out atheists who have opted for such a funeral, but demand is growing as people become more and more disillusioned with the usual 'off-the-peg', vicar service. In some parts of the British Isles, notably the West Midlands and central Scotland, funeral directors have agreed to carry publicity leaflets advertising a secular alternative. But don't think it's going to cost any less; in fact, it could well cost more, because it often entails a long journey for the officiant to perform one ceremony.

The British Humanist Association have produced a booklet entitled *Funerals Without God*, by Jane Wynn Wilson, who is one of their officiants. Of course, as it may be necessary to stress, a funeral without God is not in itself a funeral without undertakers. For this you will still have to make your own arrangements. However, if you and friends decide to conduct the ceremony yourselves, you will find *Funerals Without God* very helpful. The association have more requests for officiants than they can cope with, although they do their best. (Their address and details are on p.175.)

So, what of the future for our mortal remains or rather for the disposal thereof? Perhaps it will see the establishment of funeral societies whereby, for a minimal membership fee plus, possibly, a small annual subscription to cover the cost of leaflets, postage and telephone etc, the organizers could bargain with one or more local funeral directors for a really basic, cost-cutting affair. It might possibly include certain deductions if, for instance, a family provided its own bearers and/or transport and refused embalming etc.

There are indeed two local authorities in London who already offer a simple, low-cost funeral, arranged by negotiation with local funeral directors, and Leicester Council are looking into the possibilities of doing likewise. Also I see that council officers at Sandwell, Wolverhampton, are considering dispensing advice on DIY funerals. These are small steps in the right direction, although, of course, they are available only to local residents.

Or, even simpler and cheaper, those wishing to do their own undertaking could form groups with reciprocal motivation – 'You funeralize me and I'll funeralize you!' It's certainly worth considering.

I emphasize yet again that I know it will be only a minority who will want to take advantage of such schemes, for many reasons and for some time to come. The rest will prefer to use the professionals, who, I notice from advertisements, often state that they offer 'a truly personal, caring and compassionate service'. I hope they do. To me, a truly personal, caring and compassionate service was that given to Nigel during the latter stages of his life, which was extended, quite naturally, into the early stages of his death.

And if there's anybody there, and one of you answers to the name of Nigel Lawrence Spottiswoode – how was it for you?

8 A Report: Bang or Whimper?

'Funeral (n): A pageant whereby we attest our respect for the dead by enriching the undertaker, and strengthen our grief by an expenditure that deepens our groans and doubles our tears.' So wrote Ambrose Bierce in his *Devil's Dictionary*, published in 1891.

The Office of Fair Trading has recently published a report on funerals (which can be obtained direct from them at their address on p.174). It was compiled in response to complaints about prices charged for funerals, from the public and from MPs. 893 people who had arranged a funeral in March 1987 were interviewed and the survey's findings were augmented by letters and telephone calls to the BBC Radio 4 programme *You and Yours*.

Recommendations to the industry in the report contain many points made in this book, including that accounts should specify individually the charges for the coffin, the hearse, following cars, care and removal of body and attending to necessary arrangements. There is no suggestion that deductions should be made if the family wish to carry out some of the duties themselves, i.e. act as bearers and/or take responsibility for bringing the deceased to the funeral director's premises, and if they refuse embalming. Surely the whole premise of packaging funerals is wrong?

The report says: 'It is probably asking too much to expect funeral directors, in offering the package to their clients, to place emphasis on the fact that certain parts of it may be dispensed with.' Why? One should surely be able to see a list of all prices for specified items and, for example, to specify *that* coffin, please, and *that* lining, or no lining at all if the consumer wishes to provide his own.

A friend in London actually did some comparative shopping for a funeral a few years ago. The circumstances were as follows. Her mother, a very determined lady, had decided that she was going to die, and my friend, who had great respect for her mother's ability to get her own way, developed over many years, in obedience to her wishes (she had stated that funerals were a waste of money, and a herring-box was good enough for her) set off to sort out the cheapest possible arrangements obtainable locally. Upon enquiry, a large, expensively produced tome was presented, showing what seemed to my friend very costly merchandise. She asked if there were nothing cheaper, whereupon another, thinner book appeared from under a little lace tablecloth, accompanied by some not too subtle blackmail on the part of the undertaker along the lines that she really should spend as much as she could possibly afford, otherwise people might think that she didn't love her mother and didn't care. I am happy to report that the lady on behalf of whom the experiment was carried out is still alive and well. My friend says that she must have changed her mind, as she can't believe that she failed in any matter of strength of will!

The OFT report encourages shopping around to compare prices but also realizes the practical and emotional difficulties involved at such a time by stating that, 'Death in a world of uncertain beliefs has become something of a taboo', and certainly people do tend to think it morbid to make preparations ahead. This taboo, of course, works very much in favour of the funeral industry, who would be loath to see a more open and practical attitude. The desire to get it over with, pay up and forget, seems inherent in much of our society and may account for the surprising number of people

interviewed for the survey who said that they didn't mind
not having been given much information on prices. Only
twenty per cent said they would have liked more.

Of those who said they would have liked more
information, one continued, 'I was only shown the price of
the coffin. Later I was to receive an estimate that
included two further items, and it didn't include other
payments.' Another said, 'There was no visual pricing on
anything. We were ... embarrassed about having to ask
the price of everything.'

The report also states that, 'In some parts of the
country funeral directors think that their clients would
feel insulted if they gave them a written estimate.'
Evidence for this belief, however, is not quoted, and the
report continues:

> There are few markets where price information is so hard
> to come by. The National Association of Funeral Directors
> issues a code of practice to all its members and requires
> clients to be given a price list and a written estimate.
> Even if these requirements were complied with, and the
> evidence of our survey is that by and large they are not,
> the information probably comes too late. Also not all
> undertakers are members of the Association. Very few
> people shop around (only 3 per cent of our survey), and
> once they approach a funeral director the funeral is
> effectively sold.

Although it is stated that £800–£900 per disposal is quite
common these days, many people seem to feel that the
expense is inevitable and just shrug it off, but some,
especially the old, are angered by it. 'Several elderly
people wrote to *You and Yours* to advocate a basic body
disposal service or to ask how they could avoid having a
funeral at all.' The recommendation of the Office is that
funeral directors should allow all those who come into
immediate contact with the recently bereaved, such as
doctors, hospitals and registrars, to hold a supply of their
price lists. The need, they maintain, is for comparative

information: 'It is not enough to say, "Most people use so and so".' A spokesman for the Co-op, speaking on the report, greatly disapproved of this idea. Well, he would, wouldn't he? But it would, in fact, be immensely helpful to those stalwart souls who tend to want to shop around but for whom pressure of time forbids such activity, and also to those too bashful to ask about costs. Also in country districts there may well be twenty-five miles or more between undertakers, and as I have already explained, I have yet to find one who is prepared to quote over the telephone. Your fingers may do the walking, but the rest of you won't get far.

This is something that I wish had been taken up by the report, as it is heavily loaded on the side of the industry and if discouraged would do much to stimulate competition. In no other business will you find such coyness. The impression given is that the subject is too delicate and complicated to be discussed on the phone, when it is, in fact, no different in kind from any other monetary transaction. Who, for instance, would consider buying a dress or suit without a look at the price tag? All service industries should be regarded in exactly the same light. As is remarked by the report. 'Demand is shaped by the industry. There are formidable barriers of ignorance and reticence which prevent people considering what kind of funeral they want.'

Further on costs, the report found that the average price charged for a funeral was £586, an increase of twenty-eight per cent above the rate of inflation since 1975. Howard Hodgson dismissed the OFT's figures. He insisted that an average funeral now costs roughly three times the average weekly wage, whereas in 1945 the figure would be nine times. So, take your pick; and the first three correct answers opened will win my grateful thanks.

It is stated that around 650,000 people die each year in the United Kingdom and that, by and large, that figure is falling. If one believes the funeral companies, the only way to keep their heads above water is to expand by way of takeovers of more and more small businesses and wait for better times. The death rate is expected to rise again before the end of the century, as the population is ageing and, as mentioned earlier, the first generation whose lives were saved and continue to be saved by antibiotics must nevertheless go the way of all flesh in the next decade or two. So dry your eyes, undertakers one and all, the Great Reaper will bring home the harvest ere long.

Meanwhile some keep the temporary wolf from the door by buying up cemeteries, crematoria and florists. The trade journals at present carry many advertisements from large funeral companies eager to acquire new businesses. When this happens, the original name of the firm often remains unaltered. It is only by looking at the small print that the public may discover that the old-established firm of Deathly & Deadend is now a member of such-and-such a group.

Of the sample group of 661 people who were asked if they had paid roughly what they had expected, 472 people said that they had paid about the right amount and 132 said they had paid more than they expected. Five said less and fifty-two didn't know.

Those who paid more were then asked if the bill had included items not required. Ten said that it had. The items most often specified in this respect were bearers, following cars, embalming and use of chapel of rest. The last item should, in my opinion, be paid for only if any friend or relation wishes to view the body, because otherwise the deceased should be put in a 'pending-disposal' room, which should be included in the service.

For some time the big four who supply the majority of us with our death ceremonies have been the Co-op, the Great Southern group, Hodgson Holdings and Kenyons. The two last now having merged leaves three. Kenyons have for a long time staged the royal funerals and also had the contract for dealing with the dead in major disasters. This is a difficult and gruesome task and more complicated than many realize. I didn't myself until, quite recently, I met an ex-employee of the company. It includes the uncongenial task of identifying victims, sometimes with the minimum of identifiable evidence. Dental records may have to be checked, along with such items as wedding rings, which may often be almost all the pathologists have to go on. This is a contract that may well be coveted but also, I would suggest, in the eyes of the general public, totally unenviable – one which, my informant tells me, is carried out painstakingly and with great integrity.

The OFT report was widely reviewed in the press. As usual, on the 'good news is no news' principle, the most disparaging aspects received the most publicity. Even the report itself, after admitting that a sizeable majority were perfectly satisfied with the funeral they had arranged, seemed to concentrate more heavily on the dissatisfaction of the minority, although that may have been due to the format of the interview. For instance, when asked 'Were you satisfied or dissatisfied with the way the funeral you had arranged was conducted,' the satisfied had little to add, but the survey does report that some elaborated, and quoted three examples, of which the following is typical: 'He was marvellous – he took all the pressure off ... all we had to do was pay the bill.' The dissatisfied were questioned further and were vociferous in their displeasure.

In noting the imbalance, however, it is necessary to remember that no one enjoys a funeral, and neither the press nor the compilers of the report can be immune from the attitudes of the society in which we live. Some of the complaints voiced in the survey were indeed quite disturbing. Examples cited were: finding confetti in the following car, having the deceased's ashes left on the doorstep overnight, being charged an extra £10 to view a body after 5 p.m. and having a relation's body undressed before the family had left the room.

On 16 January 1989 *You and Yours* quoted from a number of letters about the undertaking fraternity – mostly critical. Particular comment was made regarding the high cost of funerals for babies and small children, and the insensitive handling of stillborn and short-lived infants.

Surprisingly perhaps, the report suggests that one of
the problems is that few people bother to complain.
Examples of dissatisfied clients' reasons for not
complaining are as follows: 'You just have to accept the
cost of these things. You're so upset at the time that you
don't think of such things as complaining about prices.' 'I
just didn't want to make a scene. It's paid and that's all
there is to it. It's finished with now.' 'It had to be done so I
just had to get it over and done with.' One respondent,
who was deeply upset by the casual and flippant manner
of the girl at the funeral parlour where arrangements
were being discussed, said, 'Obviously I was distraught
and would have walked out except that I couldn't start
going through it again at another undertakers ... I felt
there was no point [in complaining]. It was a situation I
couldn't be in again. I just wanted to forget the whole
business. I'd never recommend them to anyone or ever go
there again!' The report states that the Office was unable
to ascertain in this and some other cases whether the
undertaker concerned was a member of the NAFD or not,
but recommends that all funeral directors should
exercise the greatest care in the selection and training of
their staff.

The 'just want to forget it' attitude seemed to be very
prevalent. We all know what a hassle it is complaining
about anything. The excuses and buck-passing with
which one's complaint will be met often deter one from
even trying, and to complain about a funeral, particularly that it didn't appear to be good value for money, will
make many hesitate, because they feel that they may be
thought of as cheeseparing in their love and respect as
well as their cash. This feeling is something that the
industry is very conscious of, and unscrupulous
undertakers will use it to their advantage. This was
pointed out by the last-quoted correspondent: 'It was this
girl at the undertakers, who made me feel I should have a
more expensive funeral ... that I wasn't doing justice to
my Mum.'

In contrast, a woman who contacted me after my

Punters broadcast wrote: 'I worked for a short while with a
funeral directors firm. It was expensive to say the least,
and at times left a lot to be desired. I always pushed the
cheapest basic funeral with the least frills, etc. It seemed
appropriate to me at any rate because if the family looked
hard up and if the box is going to be burned or buried
anyway – who's bothered. I did not like the idea of little old
ladies going without decent food and warmth in order to
give whoever an expensive traditional send off.' Sen-
timental certainly, but also sensitive and compassionate.
I met another like her quite recently and don't doubt there
are some more around. But, to be realistic, it's unlikely
that many are going to be very vociferous in their concern,
as an employee suggesting that there is in the shop
something cheaper and equally effective is not perhaps
going to be in that particular employment for very long.

On the subject of prices, the Independent Order of Odd
Fellows has been quick to respond to the OFT report with
one of their own. The Odd Fellows are a friendly society
formed nearly 200 years ago mainly to provide savings
plans for burials. Their periodic report *The Living and the
Dead* can be obtained from their address on p.174. They
questioned a number of undertakers, none of whom
quoted the basic price of £408 plus disbursements set by
the NAFD and OFT.

These extras, mostly unavoidable, include the cost of a
burial plot or crematorium fees, minister's and church
fees, extra cars, ashes casket and grave-diggers' wages.
These additions, the Odd Fellows' report says, add about
£216 to the average cost of a burial of £520, and £103 to the
basic cremation price of £497. Of course, if you want a
higher-quality coffin, the cost can escalate by many hundreds of pounds. For customers who regard funerals as a
status symbol, it is now possible to have solid bronze
caskets shipped over from the States that will also *weigh*
many hundreds of pounds, which causes more than a little
consternation not only among the long-suffering pall-
bearers but also the funeral directors, who, fearful for the
springs of their hearses, do not, in spite of extra profit

margins, encourage the import.

Howard Hodgson, in spite of his assertions that funerals are a better bargain now than they were a decade or three ago, has nevertheless responded pretty smartly to the OFT's figures, i.e. that the cost has risen over twelve years by twenty-eight per cent more than the Retail Price Index. He nevertheless launched his own scheme, which he calls 'Dignity in Destiny', which allows funerals to be paid for in advance, either with a lump sum or by instalments. The prices range from £585 for the 'budget' version to £1,440 for the de luxe. But that does include liveried pall-bearers and chauffeur!

The mid-1989 Hodgson Holdings and Kenyon Securities merger also gave the French funeral firm Pompes Funèbres Générales a twenty-five per cent holding in the new group. Pompes Funèbres is part of the Lyonnaise des Eaux group, which has of late been buying up British water companies. PFG, which accounts for about forty-two per cent of the French home market, is already thought to be the biggest funeral concern in Europe, if not the world.

Two questions spring to mind. Is this a move that the Monopolies Commission should investigate, and are we in Britain shortly going to be offered the facility of the rock-bottom funeral price of £140 which is compulsory in France? Further information would be welcome.

However, returning to the matter of complaints, anyone feeling strong enough after the double shock of bereavement and the funeral bill does have some recourse to redress. The NAFD code of practice provides a four-step procedure designed to resolve problems.

Step I   Client contact funeral director.

Step II   If still dissatisfied, either party may consult and should co-operate with local advice centres, i.e. Citizens Advice Bureau, Consumer Advice Centre or Trading Standards Department.

Step III   The NAFD offer conciliation services at
             national level.
Step IV   If no agreement can be reached, the
             aggrieved client can go to independent
             arbitration by the Chartered Institute of
             Arbitrators. (N.B: clients may at any time
             prior to arbitration refer disputes to sheriff
             or county court.)

All this sounds fairly simple and straightforward, but
apart from the fact that by no means all funeral directors
are members of the NAFD and also that it is a
self-governing body, again the psychological and
emotional barriers inherent in the transaction often
militate against complaining. One member of the public,
who telephoned *You and Yours*, complained that she had
been told it was a 'National Association requirement'
that she pay for a following car even if it were not used.
One thing is certain: anyone complaining that funerals in
general, however packaged, are too expensive will not get
far.

The survey points to the fact that there were fewer
complaints about NAFD members (who represent eighty
per cent of the trade) than non-members. However,
Graham Barber, who is the vice-president of the
association, although professing himself 'appalled' by
some of the report's findings, admits there is little the
association can do to enforce its principles.

Bruce McDougall, who is general manager of CWS.
Funeral Services, says, 'The public is often exploited by
the cowboys of the trade.' He adds that anyone can start
up a business with just a telephone in their front room,
wait for a booking and then set about organizing it. This
confirms what Richard Buckley had already told me.
Surely, even in the present political climate which
encourages free enterprise, something must be done to
regulate the industry? My friend the outspoken Richard
Buckley said laconically, 'They've asked the wrong
people. They should have asked people who have worked

in the funeral business.'

It is necessary to stress here that neither the recommendations of the OFT nor the Code of Practice issued by the NAFD have any legal standing, and there is, as yet, no move to bring the industry to heel by law. Nevertheless, the concluding section of the report does call for a reassessment of the industry with the accent on consumer protection and with a threat of outside intervention if changes do not take place. One possibility mentioned is reference to the Monopolies and Mergers Commission. One can only await future moves with interest.

However, four months into that six-month deadline, on 21 April 1989, the *Brighton Evening Argos* published an in-depth report of an investigation by a staff journalist, posing as having a terminally ill relation, on the prices quoted to her by six local funeral directors. Rebecca Hardy says, 'My findings and my treatment raise serious questions.' Her experience included: being refused price lists by all but one firm, making it impossible to shop around as recommended by the OFT, and finding that, if you push them hard, they will offer almost identical funeral services at knock-down prices. One undercut their own basic funeral price by £200 but 'only after I had rejected all the others as too expensive'. One company refused a written estimate until a firm booking had been made, and another said, 'We do have a price list but it's not on public display. I do not know many funeral directors today who do display one.' Another said, 'We do not offer price lists. It is not compulsory. The Office of Fair Trading may recommend it but they can't make us show prices.' He added, 'We are not members of the NAFD and are not bound by its code.' This turned out to be untrue. The business concerned belonged to the Hodgson Group and *is* a member. Their regional director, when challenged, said: 'The lady you first spoke to was new. We do offer price lists.'

The turnover in counter staff seems to be above average in the funeral business. The Co-op Funeral

Services manager also described as 'a new member of our staff' a young lady who told Ms Hardy, 'You'll need a solid wood coffin, otherwise it will split open as soon as they throw the dirt on.' The manager, Ron Elphick, overturned that advice. He said what had been meant was that it was 'preferable'. Preferable by whom, one wonders? Certainly the company, although they make a good-enough profit on the veneered chipboard types also, which are perfectly satisfactory for either burials or cremations.

Only one of the companies approached would quote coffin prices separately. These ranged from £130 to £2,750, although in 1986 an investigation by the Monopolies and Mergers Commission revealed that the cost of wholesale coffins was then from £33 to £375!

Peter Martin, the president of the Sussex Association of Funeral Directors, professed himself dismayed. He said, 'Price lists should be on display in every funeral parlour. I am disappointed to learn that they are not. I thought we had improved the situation.'

It is becoming blindingly obvious that the funeral trade is still hoping that the OFT report is a temporary ripple in the smooth sea of undisturbed profit and that if they ignore its recommendations it will just go away. They may well be proved right. Their greatest ally is the public's wish to remain in ignorance of the one finite reality until 'the time comes'.

While accepting that everyone is in business for profit, further interesting questions were unearthed by Ms Hardy. For instance, how is it that a cremation arranged by a hospital for a destitute without traceable kin costs at most £150, this sum *including* cremation fees of £20, £24 for a minister, £47 for doctors' certificates, a funeral director's duties and the cost of a coffin? The cheapest price for the same funeral in the area researched was quoted at £357, the only additional facility being the use of the hearse. Given that a considerable part of the undertaker's account is simply local authority charges passed on, why do council-run crematoria charge £87 for a cremation arranged by a private individual through a funeral director and only £20 for a hospital welfare funeral? And cemeteries, some of them run by local authorities, charge £255 for a burial but only £40 to a hospital?

The survey by the *Evening Argos* has aroused predictable outrage from the undertakers that their Unofficial Secrets Act has been exposed. One of the firms interviewed accused the *Argos* of 'deceit and under-handedness'.

As for the Office of Fair Trading, it asked for a copy of the Brighton report. Its response should show whether, after baring its teeth, it really has the power to bite.

The Office of Fair Trading's report did not ignore the DIY scene, and for those interested in bypassing the industry there are a couple of short paragraphs on the subject. They note that, 'A few members of the public have dispensed with the services of a funeral director altogether, either by buying a coffin from a manufacturer or funeral director prepared to sell to the public [any such please get in touch with me – I'd be delighted to hear from them] or buying the materials and making it themselves. At least one trader retails a do-it-yourself coffin kit. There is no requirement in law for a coffin to be used for burial or cremation and some ethnic groups do not use them at all.' Incidentally, under the heading of 'Not many people know that', Frederick the Great banned the use of coffins in Prussia to save timber for the war effort!

In a later section it is remarked that,

Although most people, whose responsibility it was to arrange a funeral, felt free to arrange the type of funeral they wanted, the choice was from a relatively narrow range of options – that presented by the funeral director. Most people do not question the need to have a ceremony (with or without a minister of religion) or a coffin or a limousine, but the reason for this could well be that they do not think about the matter or feel there is no real choice. They may feel that moral, social or even legal pressures require a funeral to be organized in a particular way. They may also not question or think about the nature of the component parts of the funeral arranged by the funeral director – with the results, for example, that there may be an uncomfortable uncertainty of purpose surrounding the burial or cremation service itself.

One woman responding to the survey who had specified cremation was amazed that there was no service provided automatically, the funeral director not having discussed the arrangements with her. I myself did not realize that the last speaker must, from the pulpit, press a button to send the coffin on its way. Luckily Alan did, and in any case the last speaker was the retired reverend, who must have pressed many in his time.

Referring again to the DIY aspect of the report, it reads,

> A few people may even prefer a more radical approach. Funeral directors committed to, and taking pride in, what they feel is the 'traditional' style of funeral would probably be affronted by the letter sent to 'You and Yours', which said, 'Personally, I'd settle for a plastic bag for what is left of me after my "donated" parts have been removed.' The office believes that the writer of this letter has as much right to have her wishes respected, provided there is no conflict within the law, as someone who wants a solid oak coffin: *consumers are under no obligation to modify their wishes to meet the aspirations of traders in this or any other field*. The Office does not seek to advocate plastic bag disposal or home-made coffins; its concern is that information about options such as these should be available to members of the public and that nothing should stop people having them if that is what they want.

Well, thanks a lot, OFT. I and other renegades are truly grateful for your support. In my turn it would be only fair to point out that, given the knowledge, most people will still opt for, and even need, the more traditional rites and rituals. At a time of distress they can be reassuring and give considerable consolation to the bereaved, provided, of course, they are carried out in a satisfactory manner.

A funeral is no one's idea of a treat, and no one will ever love a funeral director (except, of course, we hope, his wife and family). Universal popularity is, by the nature of their trade, not for them. But the fact that some of them take us for a ride when we are bewildered by grief, riddled with guilt or overwhelmed by remorse is, in part, our own fault for so resolutely turning away from the notion of our own mortality. As Stephen Pile put it in his excellent review of the report in *The Sunday Times* of 15 January 1989, 'If funerals are costly it is not the undertakers' fault, but ours. We are so cut off from reality that we cannot cope with death any more than we can kill the animals we eat or give birth to our children without drugs; (midwives tell me that at the present rate, Caesarean births will become the norm and natural labour will be lost).'

In the Spring of 1990 a new code of practice was agreed between the OFT and the NAFD in which was included the undertaking to display prominently in their offices the price of their basic (i.e. cheapest) funeral, but the Association would not concede to an itemization of the components. Nevertheless it is a step in the right direction and it will be interesting to see if all NAFD members will adhere to it.

Funeral directors recognize that their profession is vulnerable. 'They make jokes about us,' says Michael Kenyon sadly. Yes, we do, but then we always joke about what we fear, and the greater the taboo surrounding that fear, the louder the laughter. But Michael Kenyon continues, 'People are beginning to realize that we are a service industry that everyone is going to need at some stage.' Not so, Mr Kenyon, and not Nigel. We did very nicely, thank you, without it.

Postscript

On the anniversary of Nigel's death, Joy, Alan and I went to dinner at a country-house hotel near Llandudno. It was a perfect evening. The weather was clement for a change, the food and service left nothing to be desired and, as always, we enjoyed each other's company. It was two in the morning before I got home, and I was wakened before eight by the telephone. A rather distracted-sounding lady wished to enquire about my coffins.

'My what?' I said.

'Oh, I'm so sorry,' came the answer. 'I have so many names and numbers written down here. Oh dear, I must have made a mistake.' She was palpably greatly embarrassed and about to ring off.

I was wide awake now. 'No, hold on a moment,' I said. 'I think I know what you're talking about.'

I was right. She had heard my broadcast and wanted the name of the firm who had supplied Nigel's coffin. Her husband had died the day before, and she and her family were determined that he should not be taken from them to the anonymity of a funeral home, and themselves wanted to make all the arrangements. I told her that, sadly, S. & S. Joinery were no longer supplying the public, and put her in touch with my Gainsborough contact, Steve Nicholson. I understand that her brother drove up from London and brought one back that day.

A week later I telephoned her to ask if all had gone as she wished. She said that it had, and added, 'It was a wonderful feeling, and I'll always be deeply glad that we succeeded in doing it our way.'

And that was nice, wasn't it?

Useful Addresses

To bequeath one's body for medical research
(In England and Wales)
HM Inspector of Anatomy
DHSS
Eileen House
80–94 Newington Causeway
SE1 6EF

(In Scotland)
Scottish Home and Health Department
St Andrews House
Edinburgh EH1 3DE

For burial at sea
The Fisheries Inspectorate
MAFF
Great Westminster House
Horseferry Road
London SW1P 2AE

To arrange a funeral without using a funeral director:
Age Concern
Astral House
1268 London Road
London SW16 4ER Tel: 081 679 8000
(Ask for the fact sheet *Arranging a Funeral*)

Retail coffins:
James Gibson
134 Darwen Street
Blackburn
Lancs. Tel: Blackburn 681500

Complaints about members of the NAFD:
The National Secretary
National Association of Funeral Directors
618 Warwick Road
Solihull
West Midlands B91 1AA

To obtain free copy of The Living and the Dead.
The Independent Order of Odd Fellows
Odd Fellows House
40 Fountain Street
Manchester M2 2AB
(SAE appreciated)

For body bags:
Lear of London
Bryson House
Horace Road
Kingston Upon Thames
Surrey KT1 2SL Tel: 081 546 2663

Office of Fair Trading
Field House
15-25 Breams Buildings
London EC4A 1PR Tel: 081 242 2858

For the book *Funerals without God*
The British Humanist Association
14 Lambs Conduit Passage
London W8 5PG Tel: 071 430 0908

For *What To Do When Someone Dies* and *Wills and Probate*
The Consumers Association
2 Marylebone Road
London NW1 4DX Tel: 081 486 5544

The Natural Death Centre
20 Heber Road
London NW2 6AA Tel: 081 208 2853

Notes to Paperback Edition

In January 1991 Howard Hodgson left the funeral business 'to pursue other interests'. One of these is the authorship of a book, *How To Become Dead Rich*.

On 14 April 1991 The Natural Death Centre was launched. Its overall aim is 'To help improve the quality of dying.' They hold regular dinners and discussions on all aspects of the subject, and also seem to be acting as an effective pressure group. For instance, in giving a great deal of publicity to the funeral directors' practice of refusing to sell a coffin by itself. Some funeral directors will now agree to do so but a minimum price quoted of around £300 will be unlikely to greatly appeal to DIY undertakers. Nicholas Albery, the centre's director, also conducted a survey of prices through its members. One contact offered an undertaker £400 in cash for a £795 funeral and was accepted.

In mid October 1991 Edward Leigh, Minister for Consumer Affairs, announced that he had 'asked the NAFD to amend their code of practice to require their members to provide itemised estimates of their charges for funeral services'. The Association seems to be in no hurry to answer this request. As I write (March 1992) according to my information from the Department of Trade and Industry this does not appear to have been agreed.